Developing Numeracy
NUMBERS AND THE NUMBER SYSTEM
ACTIVITIES FOR THE DAILY MATHS LESSON

year 5

Hilary Koll and Steve Mills

A & C BLACK

Contents

Reprinted 2000, 2002 (twice)
Published 2000 by A&C Black Publishers Limited
37 Soho Square, London W1D 3QZ
www.acblack.com

ISBN O-7136-5235-7

Copyright text © Hilary Koll and Steve Mills, 2000
Copyright illustrations © Gaynor Berry, 2000
Copyright cover illustration © Charlotte Hard 2000

The authors and publisher would like to thank the following teachers for their advice in producing this series of books:
Tracy Adam; Shilpa Bharambe; Hardip Channa; Sue Hall; Ann Hart; Lydia Hunt; Madeleine Madden; Helen Mason;
Anne Norbury; Jane Siddons; Judith Wells; Fleur Whatley.

A CIP catalogue record for this book is available from the British Library.

A & C Black uses paper produced with elemental chlorine-free pulp, harvested from managed sustainable forests.

Printed in Great Britain by St Edmundsbury Press Ltd, Bury St Edmunds, Suffolk.

Introduction

Developing Numeracy: Numbers and the Number System is a series of seven photocopiable activity books designed to be used during the daily maths lesson. The books focus on the first strand of the National Numeracy Strategy *Framework for teaching mathematics*. The activities are intended to be used during the time allocated to pupil activities; they aim to reinforce the teaching within the lesson and provide practice and consolidation of the objectives contained in the framework document.

Year 5 supports the teaching of mathematics to Year 5 children by providing a series of activities to develop and reinforce essential skills in number work. The activities relate to place value, ordering and rounding; properties of numbers and number sequences; and fractions, decimals and percentages, ratio and proportion. They build on the children's understanding of the concepts taught in Year 4 and also introduce –

- ordering a set of positive and negative integers;
- counting in steps of 0·1, 0·2 etc., extending beyond zero when counting back;
- knowing squares of numbers to at least 10 x 10;
- finding all the pairs of factors of any number up to 100;
- solving simple problems using ideas of ratio and proportion;
- rounding a number with one or two decimal places to the nearest integer;
- using division to find simple fractions of numbers and quantities;
- beginning to understand percentages, and finding simple percentages of small quantities.

Extension

Many of the activity sheets end with a challenge (**Now try this!**) which reinforces and extends the children's learning, and provides the teacher with the opportunity for assessment. Where children are asked to carry out an activity, the instructions are clear to enable them to work independently although the teacher may wish to read out the instructions and provide further support where necessary. The children may need to write their answers on a separate sheet of paper.

Organisation

For some of the activities it will be useful to have available coloured pencils, calculators, scissors (for cutting out activities), number lines (including negative numbers), place value cards (sometimes called arrow cards) and 100-squares. To help teachers to select appropriate learning experiences for their children the activities are grouped into sections within each book. The pages are not intended to be presented in the order in which they appear unless otherwise stated.

Teachers' notes

Very brief notes are provided at the end of most pages, giving ideas and suggestions for maximising the effectiveness of the activity sheets. These notes could be masked before photocopying.

Structure of the daily maths lesson

The recommended structure of the daily maths lesson for Key Stage 2 is as follows:

Start to lesson, oral work, mental calculation	5–10 minutes
Main teaching and pupil activities	about 40 minutes
Plenary	about 10 minutes

Each lesson should include:
- a pacey start with the whole class involved in counting, oral and mental calculation work;
- some direct interactive teaching of the whole class on the maths objective for the day;
- group or individual activities linked to the objective of the lesson. The teacher should focus on one group to continue teaching directly. The activities in the **Developing Numeracy** books are designed to be carried out in the time allocated to group activities;
- a plenary with the whole class after the group activities are ended to consolidate and extend the children's learning through questions and discussion.

The following chart shows an example of the way in which an activity from this book can be used to achieve the required organisation of the daily maths lesson for Year 5 children.

Earth facts (page 21)

Start to the lesson Begin by asking the children to count out the multiples of 1000 from zero, for example: 1000, 2000, 3000… up to 10000. Write these numbers on the board and label them 'Multiples of 1000'. Ask the children what the multiples of 1000 have in common. (They have at least three zeros at the end.) Point out that 10 000 is a multiple of 1000 with four zeros. Ask the children to count out the multiples of 100, starting from 1000, for example: 1100, 1200, 1300, 1400, 1500… up to 3000. List some of these on the board. Ask the children what the multiples of 100 have in common. (They have at least two zeros at the end.) Now invite the class to count out the multiples of 10 above 2300, for example: 2310, 2320, 2330, 2340… Ask the children to identify what the multiples of 10 have in common. (They have at least one zero at the end.) List some numbers that are multiples of 10, 100 or 1000, for example: 2000, 2330, 2400. Ask questions such as: "*Is 2000 a multiple of 10? of 100? of 1000?*" Ensure that the children can recognise multiples of 10, 100 and 1000 before moving on.	**5–10 minutes**

Main teaching and pupil activities Explain that the children will be 'rounding' numbers. Ask them to describe the meaning of the word rounding (finding to which multiple of 10, 100 or 1000 a number is closest). Show or draw a number line segment from 1289–1310 with the multiples of 10 marked on it.	**about 40 minutes**

```
1290              1300              1310
|--+--+--+--+--+--+--+--|--+--+--+--+--+--+--+--|
```

Point to positions on the line and ask children to identify the numbers between the multiples of 10, for example: 1291, 1307. For each number, ask the children to identify the multiple of 10 to which it is closest. Explain that this is rounding to the nearest 10. Tell the children that if they are rounding to the nearest 100, the answer will always be a multiple of 100, that is, it will have at least two zeros at the end. Remind them that 5s normally round up. Give some numbers between 2000 and 4000 and ask the children to round them to the nearest 100, for example, 2387 will round to 2400. Remind them that 50s round up. Repeat for multiples of 1000, reminding the children that 500s normally round up, for example, 2500 rounds to 3000. The children could then work on **Earth facts** (page 21, **Developing Numeracy: Numbers and the Number System Year 5**).

Plenary Discuss the children's answers and go over a few examples on the board. Ask the children to check that each answer in a column has the correct number of zeros at the end (that in the first column all the numbers have at least one zero at the end, and in the second column at least two zeros).	**about 10 minutes**

Further activities

The following activities provide some practical ideas for whole class mental and oral work. These are intended to introduce or reinforce the main teaching part of the lesson.

Place value, ordering and rounding

Show me
Each child has a set of digit cards from 0 to 9. Play 'show me' activities where each child shows a number by holding one or two digit cards in the air as you say, "*Show me the number 18 rounded to the nearest 10… a multiple of 7… a number divisible by 5*" and so on. You can adapt the game to support teaching about place value by writing a decimal (for example, 6·3) on the board and saying to the children, "*Show me how many units and how many tenths.*"

People numbers

Invite ten children to the front. Give each child a card with a two or three-digit number on it to hold in front of them, facing the class, and ask the ten children to order themselves from highest to lowest. Then invite individual children from the rest of the class to change places with those at the front, for example: *"Jo change places with a number divisible by four; Daniel change places with a multiple of nine."*

Totals

Draw a 'dartboard' as shown. Ask the children to imagine that they have three darts, then set them challenges such as: *"What is the closest score you can make to 16, 83, 349, 856? How many different scores between 600 and 650 can you make? How many numbers over 2000 can you make?"*

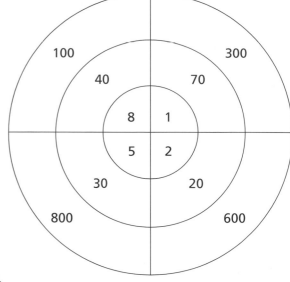

Properties of numbers and number sequences

Counting stick

Hold the stick (which could be a metre stick with every 10 cm coloured) so that all the children can see it. Decide on a number (for example, eight) and ask children to count in eights as you point to each coloured section in turn. When counting back, extend beyond zero. This provides practice in counting forwards and backwards and helps the children to remember the multiples of a given number.

Jumping along

Ask the children to count on or back from a given starting number, for example, backwards in 11s from 88 or forwards in 25s from −100. This game can be played in small groups or around the whole class.

Fractions, decimals and percentages, ratio and proportion

Fraction cards

Give the children a selection of fraction cards labelled $\frac{1}{10}$, $\frac{3}{20}$, $1\frac{4}{5}$, etc. Ask the children to arrange themselves in order, starting with the smallest fraction.

Decimal darts

Draw a simple dartboard with a range of decimals with two decimal places, for example, 0·02, 0·14, 0·25. Invite the children to chose two numbers and add them, then ask them to explain their answers in words.

Numbers in the environment

Discuss with the children examples of numbers that they can see and hear around them which exemplify the number work they are doing, for example: 'buy one get one free' deals in shops provide an opportunity to consider ideas of ratio and proportion in a real context.

Selected answers

p 9
numbers in figures:
  62 624
  470 917
  12 063
2 028 011
5 307 534

numbers in words:
• ninety-nine thousand, five hundred and two
• six hundred and thirty thousand and four
• two hundred and seven thousand and seventy
• four million and one
• nine million, seven hundred and eighty-one thousand, eight hundred and forty-six

p 11
	2. £600
3. £900 000	4. £20 000
5. £4 000 000	6. £3000
7. £800 000	8. £30 000

10. six million~
     6 463 075
11. two hundred thousand~
     9 275 698
12. five hundred~
     8 006 553
13. seven~
     7 559 967
14. ten~
     2 181 419

Now try this!
6 204 517

p 12
1. 4 000 000, 200 000, 0, 3000, 800, 70, 5,
2. 6 000 000, 300 000, 20 000, 5000, 700, 60, 4
3. 1 000 000, 800 000, 90 000, 1000, 600, 30, 8
5. 4 000 000 + 200 000 + 0 + 4000 + 100 + 60 + 7
6. 8 000 000 + 600 000 + 30 000 + 0 + 0 +70 + 2
7. 5 000 000 + 900 000 + 60 000 + 7000 + 0 + 0 + 6

p 13
2.	140
3.	3610
4.	527 130
5.	2800
6.	10 400
7.	26 000
8.	0

9. 10 **10.** 10 **11.** 10
12. 100 **13.** 10 **14.** 100

p 14
2. 736 000
3. 73 600
4. 7360

Now try this!
1. 100 **2.** 10 **3.** 10
4. 10 **5.** 1000 **6.** 10

6

p 15
1. 17 261
2. 173 910
3. 271 351
4. 541 070
5. 43 571
6. 79 862
7. 35 101
8. 28 127
9. 61 074
10. 114 041
11. 701 419
12. 110 140

Now try this!
1. >
2. >
3. <
4. <
5. >
6. <

p 16
1. 692, 725, 1899, 5617, 6820, 9543
2. 294, 2562, 2847, 23 645, 25 499, 29 110
3. 589, 3619, 4159, 4160, 4261, 4512

Now try this!
971601
294

p 17
2. 450 x 2
3. 54 x 02
4. 205 + 4 or 204 + 5
5. 425 − 0
6. 402 ÷ 5

Now try this!
51 + 23
513 x 2
13 x 25
215 + 3 or 213 + 5
352 − 1
153 ÷ 2

p 18
the actual number of bricks:
1. 110
2. 30
3. 50
4. 170

p 19
the actual position of the arrow on the number line:
1. 400
2. 0.2
3. 75
4. 5.8
5. 2.9
6. 10
7. −4
8. 50.3
9. −2.5
10. 7
11. −1
12. 1.6

p 20
Now try this!
1. 3500
2. 4300
3. 6400
4. 8000
5. 9800
6. 2800

p 21
volcano heights:
2. 4170 m, 4200 m, 4000 m
3. 6130 m, 6100 m, 6000 m
4. 2800 m, 2800 m, 3000 m
5. 4750 m, 4800 m, 5000 m
6. 3720 m, 3700 m, 4000 m

annual rainfalls:
1. 11 430 mm, 11 400 mm, 11 000 mm
2. 4650 mm, 4600 mm, 5000 mm
3. 4500 mm, 4500 mm, 4000 mm
4. 11 770 mm, 11 800 mm, 12 000 mm
5. 10 280 mm, 10 300 mm, 10 000 mm
6. 160 mm, 200 mm, 0 mm

p 22
1. −2
2. −6
3. −4
4. −5
5. −8
6. −6
7. −5
8. 0
9. −7, −6
10. −1, 0
11. −7, −6, −5, −4, −3, −2, −1, 0, 1, 2, 3, 4, 5
12. −20, −19, −18, −17, −16, −15, −14, −13, −12, −11, −10, −9

Now try this!
−10

p 23
2. −2 °C
3. −4 °C
4. −9 °C
5. 1 °C
6. −8 °C
7. −8 °C
8. 4 °C
9. −1 °C
10. −6 °C
11. 10 °C
12. −10 °C

Now try this!
1. 3 °C
2. 19 °C
3. 5 °C
4. 14 °C

p 24
0, 6, 12, 18, 24, 30, 36, 42, 48, 54, 60, 66, 72, 78, 84, 90
0, 7, 14, 21, 28, 35, 42, 49, 56, 63, 70, 77, 84, 91, 98
0, 8, 16, 24, 32, 40, 48, 56, 64, 72, 80, 88, 96, 104, 112
0, 9, 18, 27, 36, 45, 54, 63, 72, 81, 90, 99, 108, 117, 126, 135

paths:
96, 90, 84, 78, 72, 66, 60, 54, 48, 42, 36, 30
98, 91, 84, 77, 70, 63, 56, 49, 42, 35, 28, 21
96, 88, 80, 72, 64, 56, 48, 40, 32, 24, 16, 8
99, 90, 81, 72, 63, 54, 45, 36, 27, 18, 9, 0

Now try this!
4, 10, 16, 22, 28, 34, 40, 46, 52, 58, 64, 70, 76, 82, 88, 94, 100

p 26
Now try this!
50, 39, 28, 17, 6, -5, -16

p 27
1. 24, 32, 40, 48, 56, 64, 72, 80, 88, 96
2. 35, 42, 49, 56, 63, 70, 77, 84, 91, 98
3. 99, 90, 81, 72, 63, 54, 45, 36, 27, 18, 9, 0
4. 475, 450, 425, 400, 375, 350, 325, 300
5. 24, 30, 36, 42, 48, 54, 60, 66, 72, 78, 84, 90, 96
6. 88, 80, 72, 64, 56, 48, 40, 32, 24, 16, 8, 0
7. 0, 25, 50, 75, 100, 125, 150, 175, 200, 225
8. 0, 0.1, 0.2, 0.3, 0.4, 0.5, 0.6, 0.7, 0.8, 0.9, 1, 1.1, 1.2, 1.3, 1.4, 1.5, 1.6, 1.7, 1.8, 1.9, 2
9. 4.8, 4.7, 4.6, 4.5, 4.4, 4.3, 4.2, 4.1, 4, 3.9, 3.8, 3.7, 3.6, 3.5, 3.4, 3.3, 3.2
10. 99, 88, 77, 66, 55, 44, 33, 22, 11, 0
11. 0, 11, 22, 33, 44, 55, 66, 77, 88, 99, 110, 121, 132
12. 0, −11, −22, −33, −44, −55, −66, −77, −88
13. 2.8, 2.9, 3, 3.1, 3.2, 3.3, 3.4, 3.5, 3.6, 3.7, 3.8, 3.9, 4, 4.1, 4.2, 4.3, 4.4, 4.5, 4.6
14. 84, 77, 70, 63, 56, 49, 42, 35, 28, 21, 14, 7, 0
15. 88, 99, 110, 121, 132
16. 1, 12, 23, 34, 45, 56, 67, 78, 89, 100, 111
17. 1000, 750, 500, 250
18. −33, −22, −11, 0, 11, 22, 33, 44, 55

p 29
1. 15
2. 8
3. 42
4. 23
5. 17
6. 60
7. 18
8. 16
9. even
10. odd
11. odd
12. even
13. odd
14. even

p 32
numbers that are exactly divisible by 1 and 2
numbers that are exactly divisible by 1 and 3

The numbers in the middle are exactly divisible by 1, 2, 3 and 6

Now try this!
numbers that are exactly divisible by 2:
2, 4, 6, 8, 12, 14, 16, 18, 22, 24, 26, 28, 30
numbers that are exactly divisible by 5:
5, 15, 25, 30
numbers that are exactly divisible by 2 and 5:
10, 20, 30
numbers that are divisible by neither:
1, 3, 7, 9, 11, 13, 17, 19, 21, 23, 27, 29

p 33
LADYBIRD

p 35
2. 1 x 12, 2 x 6, 3 x 4
3. 1 x 30, 2 x 15, 3 x 10, 5 x 6
4. 1 x 32, 2 x 16, 4 x 8
5. 1 x 28, 2 x 14, 4 x 7
6. 1 x 40, 2 x 20, 4 x 10, 5 x 8

Now try this!
1 ➤ 1 x 1
4 ➤ 1 x 4, 2 x 2
9 ➤ 1 x 9, 3 x 3
16 ➤ 1 x 16, 2 x 8, 4 x 4
25 ➤ 1 x 25, 5 x 5
36 ➤ 1 x 36, 2 x 18, 3 x 12, 4 x 9, 6 x 6

p 36
1. 1, 2, 3, 4, 6, 8, 12, 24
2. 1, 2, 4, 5, 10, 20
3. 1, 2, 4, 8, 16, 32
4. 1, 2, 3, 4, 6, 8, 12, 16, 24, 48
5. 1, 2, 3, 4, 6, 8, 9, 12, 18, 24, 36, 72
6. 1, 2, 3, 4, 6, 7, 12, 14, 21, 28, 42, 84

Now try this!
60 ➤ 1, 2, 3, 4, 5, 6, 10, 12, 15, 20, 30, 60
96 ➤ 1, 2, 3, 4, 6, 8, 12, 16, 24, 32, 48, 96

p 37
improper fractions:
$\frac{14}{8}$, $\frac{15}{10}$, $1\frac{1}{5}$
mixed numbers:
$6\frac{7}{14}$, $5\frac{4}{9}$, $2\frac{4}{5}$, $3\frac{7}{8}$
fractions with a numerator of 1: $\frac{1}{9}$, $\frac{1}{10}$
proper fractions:
$\frac{4}{7}$, $\frac{1}{9}$, $\frac{1}{10}$, $\frac{6}{8}$
fractions with a denominator of 10: $\frac{1}{10}$, $\frac{7}{10}$

p 38
1. $\frac{5}{2} = 2\frac{1}{2}$
2. $\frac{12}{10} = 1\frac{2}{10}$
3. $\frac{7}{4} = 1\frac{3}{4}$
4. $\frac{11}{5} = 2\frac{1}{5}$
5. $\frac{25}{4} = 6\frac{1}{4}$
6. $\frac{17}{4} = 4\frac{1}{4}$
7. $\frac{32}{10} = 3\frac{2}{10}$
8. $\frac{41}{10} = 4\frac{1}{10}$
9. $\frac{7}{2} = 3\frac{1}{2}$

Now try this!
1. $\frac{9}{4}$ 2. $4\frac{3}{10}$ 3. $\frac{62}{10}$
4. $2\frac{2}{5}$ 5. $\frac{38}{5}$ 6. $10\frac{2}{4}$

p 39
2, 5, 8, 9, 10

Now try this!
$\frac{1}{8}$

p 40
Team 1: $\frac{1}{2}, \frac{5}{10}, \frac{3}{6}, \frac{2}{4}, \frac{4}{8}, \frac{6}{12}, \frac{50}{100}, \frac{7}{14},$

Team 2: $\frac{1}{3}, \frac{2}{6}, \frac{3}{9}, \frac{5}{15}, \frac{4}{12}, \frac{10}{30}, \frac{6}{18}, \frac{8}{24}, \frac{7}{21}$

1. $\frac{1}{4} = \frac{2}{8} = \frac{3}{12} = \frac{4}{16} = \frac{5}{20} = \frac{6}{24} = \frac{7}{28}$
2. $\frac{1}{5} = \frac{2}{10} = \frac{3}{15} = \frac{4}{20} = \frac{5}{25} = \frac{6}{30} = \frac{7}{35}$
3. $\frac{1}{10} = \frac{2}{20} = \frac{3}{30} = \frac{4}{40} = \frac{5}{50} = \frac{6}{60} = \frac{7}{70}$

p 41
3. =
6. <
9. =
12. =

Now try this!
1. >   2. <
3. <   4. <

p 43
3. $\frac{1}{8}, \frac{1}{4}, \frac{1}{2}, \frac{5}{8}, \frac{3}{4}, \frac{7}{8}$
4. $\frac{1}{10}, \frac{3}{20}, \frac{1}{4}, \frac{1}{2}, \frac{11}{20}, \frac{3}{4}, \frac{9}{10}$

Now try this!
1. <   2. <
3. <   4. <

p 45
1. one tenth of:
40 = 4, 340 = 34, 3000 = 300, 70 = 7, 6000 = 600, 900 = 90
2. one hundredth of:
1300 = 13, 600 = 6, 4000 = 40, 51000 = 510, 300 = 3, 72000 = 720
3. six tenths of:
20 = 12, 40 = 24, 600 = 360, 90 = 54, 400 = 240, 100 = 60

4. three tenths of:
100 = 30, 20 = 6, 300 = 90, 60 = 18, 50 = 150, 10 = 3
5. three quarters of:
4 = 3, 40 = 30, 24 = 18, 100 = 75, 12 = 9,
6. two hundredths of:
100 = 2, 200 = 4, 1400 = 28, 300 = 6, 4000 = 80, 700 = 14

Now try this!
• 4, 8, 12, 16, 20, 24, 28, 32, 36, 40
• 3, 6, 9, 12, 15, 18, 21, 24, 27, 30

p 46
1. 30 cm 90 cm 20 cm
2. 6 kg 30 kg 4 kg
3. 20 ml 40 ml 180 ml
4. 5 kg 15 kg 20 kg
5. 8 cm 40 cm 6 cm
6. 80 ml 160 ml 8 ml
7. 20 cm 140 cm 1800 cm
8. 7 l 21 l 10 l
9. 30 kg 35 kg 36 kg

p 47
1. $\frac{1}{100}, \frac{3}{100}, \frac{27}{100}$
2. $\frac{1}{10}, \frac{3}{10}, \frac{9}{10}$
3. $\frac{1}{1000}, \frac{35}{1000}, \frac{750}{1000}$
4. $\frac{1}{1000}, \frac{7}{1000}, \frac{99}{1000}$
(or equivalents)
5. $\frac{1}{1000}, \frac{95}{1000}, \frac{1}{2}$
6. $\frac{1}{7}, \frac{3}{7}, \frac{5}{7}$
7. $\frac{1}{24}, \frac{1}{2}, \frac{1}{4}$

Now try this!
1. 1   2. 30   3. 59
4. 1   5. 15   6. 47

p 48
1. false
2. true
3. true
4. false
5. true
6. true
7. false

p 49
1. 2 bars of soap, 4 packets of biscuits, 1 toothbrush, 5 batteries, 3 toilet rolls
2. 2 pens, 6 tapes, 12 batteries, 4 pencils, 10 books

p 50
2. 1.3 bars
3. 1.09 bars 4. 1.84 bars
5. 2.01 bars 6. 1.1 bars
7. 3.91 bars

p 51
1. 0.7 2. 0.06 3. 0.3 4. 0.01
5. 821.46 6. 131.25 7. 769.21
8. 105.79 9. 420.68
10. 3.65
11. 10.49
12. 15.07

p 53
2. 0.08
3. 0.06
4. 0.2
5. 3.0
6. 0.8
7. 0.1
8. 0.03
9. 10   10. 10
11. 100   12. 10

Now try this!
1.24

p 54
1. 5.92, 5.95, 5.99, 6.0, 6.01, 6.05, 6.09
2. 4.96, 4.99, 5, 5.02, 5.04, 5.09, 5.1
3. 0.01, 0.05, 0.06, 0.08, 0.1 0.13, 0.14

p 56
3. ✓   16. ✓
4. ✓   17. ✓
5. X (4)   18. X (15)
6. X (3)   19. ✓
7. ✓   20. ✓
8. X (10)   21. X (100)
9. X (8)   22. ✓
10. ✓   23. X (12)
11. X (7)   24. ✓
12. X (6)   25. ✓
13. X (8)   26. ✓
14. ✓   27. X (666)
15. ✓   28. ✓
             29. ✓
             30. ✓

Now try this!
3.5, 3.6, 3.7, 3.8, 3.9

p 57
1.61~2, 1.35~1, 2.70~3, 2.33~2, 4.75~5, 1.99~2, 2.41~2, 4.19~4, 5.49~5, 5.50~6, 6.54~7, 4.91~5, 6.99~7, 6.47~6, 7.29~7, 3.02~3, 4.35~4

1. 13   2. 26
3. 105   4. 133
5. 480   6. 600
7. 600   8. 799

p 59
1. 50% 2. 80% 3. 5%
4. 65% 5. 26 % 6. 63%
7. There is a number of possible answers. Ensure the percentages on the label total 100%.

p 60
1. 10% 2. 90% 3. 60% 4. 40%
5. 99% 6. 1% 7. 75% 8. 25%
9. true
10. false
11. false
12. true
13. false
14. true
15. true

p 61
2. 16
3. 44
4. 62
5. 200
6. 180
7. 250
8. 500
9. 1   10. 4   11. 10
12. 50 13. 80 14. 150
15. 6
16. 9
17. 11
18. 34
19. 690
20. 100
21. 5200
22. 30 23. 12 24. 18
25. 150 26. 450 27. 666
28. 6 29. 30 30. 170

p 64
• 0·75, $\frac{75}{100}$, $\frac{3}{4}$, three quarters, 75%
• 0·01, one per cent, 1%, $\frac{1}{100}$
• 20%, $\frac{20}{100}$, 0.2, $\frac{1}{5}$, one fifth
• 10%, 0.1, zero point one, ten per cent, one tenth, $\frac{1}{10}$
• fifty per cent, zero point five, a half, 0·50, 50%, 0·5, $\frac{1}{2}$
• 100%, $\frac{1}{1}$, one whole
• 25%, $\frac{25}{100}$, $\frac{1}{4}$, 0·25

In figures, in words

- ● **Write these numbers in figures.**

words	figures
sixty-two thousand, six hundred and twenty-four	
four hundred and seventy thousand, nine hundred and seventeen	
twelve thousand and sixty-three	
two million, twenty-eight thousand and eleven	
five million, three hundred and seven thousand, five hundred and thirty-four	

- ● **Write these numbers in words.**

figures	words
99 502	
630 004	
207 070	
4 000 001	
9 781 846	

- ● **Use the digits** 3 , 6 , 0 , 0 , 0 , 1 **and** 9
  to make five seven-digit numbers .
- ● **Write the numbers in words.**

Teachers' note Children may need to be reminded of more difficult spellings, such as forty, eighteen and ninety. Remind the children of how zero works as a place holder.

Developing Numeracy
Numbers and the Number System
Year 5
© A & C Black

Matchmaker

- **Cut out the cards.**
- **Match the figures and words.**

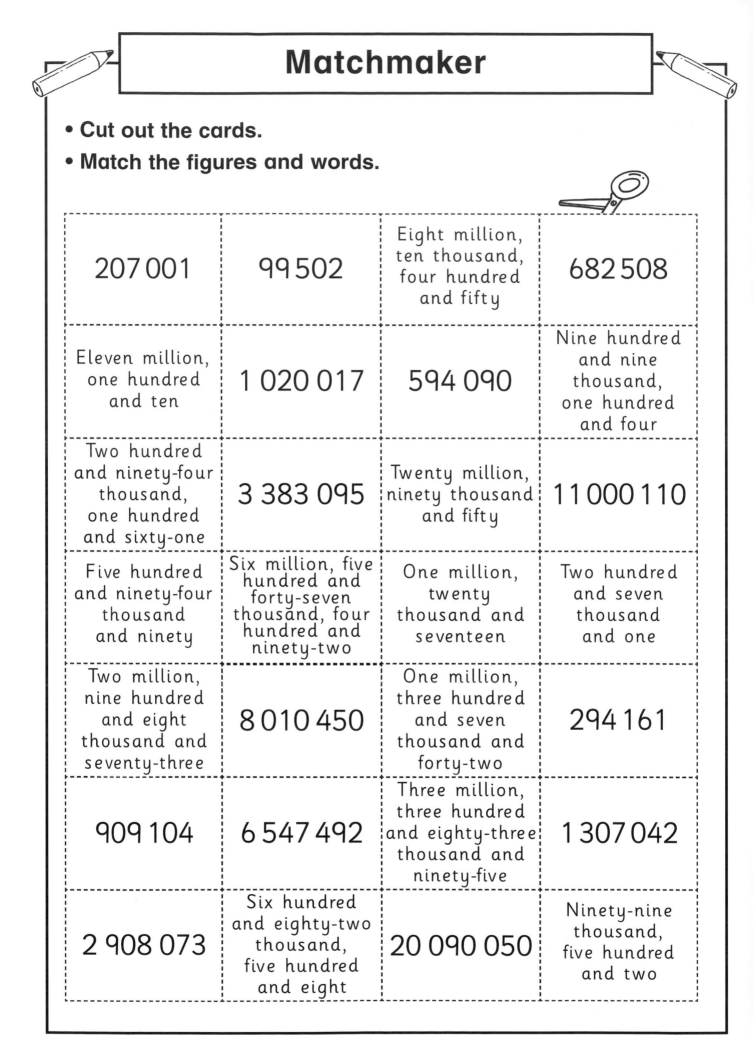

207 001	99 502	Eight million, ten thousand, four hundred and fifty	682 508
Eleven million, one hundred and ten	1 020 017	594 090	Nine hundred and nine thousand, one hundred and four
Two hundred and ninety-four thousand, one hundred and sixty-one	3 383 095	Twenty million, ninety thousand and fifty	11 000 110
Five hundred and ninety-four thousand and ninety	Six million, five hundred and forty-seven thousand, four hundred and ninety-two	One million, twenty thousand and seventeen	Two hundred and seven thousand and one
Two million, nine hundred and eight thousand and seventy-three	8 010 450	One million, three hundred and seven thousand and forty-two	294 161
909 104	6 547 492	Three million, three hundred and eighty-three thousand and ninety-five	1 307 042
2 908 073	Six hundred and eighty-two thousand, five hundred and eight	20 090 050	Ninety-nine thousand, five hundred and two

Teachers' note The cards could also be used as a whole class activity where the children could find a partner who has the same number. Encourage the children to make more cards using different numbers.

Developing Numeracy
Numbers and the Number System
Year 5
© A & C Black

Jackpot digits

- **Write the value of the underlined digit in each lottery jackpot.**

1. £25**7**960   £50 000

2. £417 6**3**1   _____

3. £7 **9**12 413   _____

4. £6 4**2**1 550   _____

5. £**4** 685 100   _____

6. £8 20**3** 125   _____

7. £1 8**5**2 964   _____

8. £3 3**3**4 286   _____

- **Read the number on each pen.**
- **Join the pen to a lid which has a digit with the same value.**

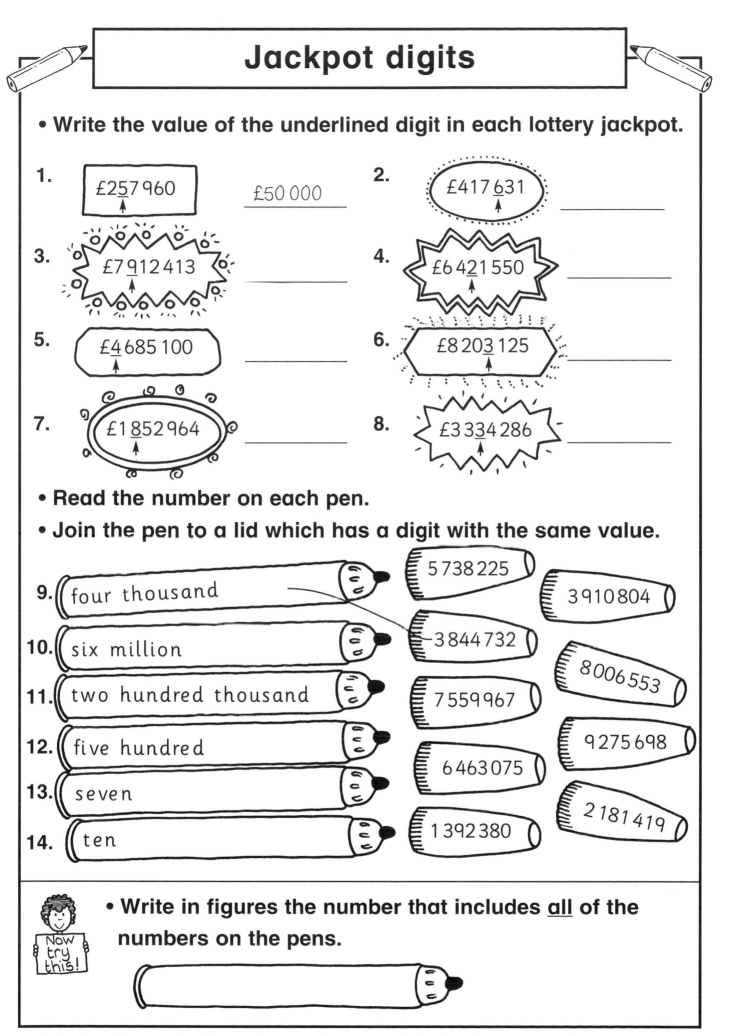

9. four thousand

10. six million

11. two hundred thousand

12. five hundred

13. seven

14. ten

Lids: 5 738 225   3 910 804   3 844 732   8 006 553   7 559 967   9 275 698   6 463 075   1 392 380   2 181 419

- **Write in figures the number that includes <u>all</u> of the numbers on the pens.**

Teachers' note Encourage the children to draw place value columns and write the numbers in to help them with these activities. Point out to the children that not all the lids are used in the second section.

Developing Numeracy
Numbers and the Number System
Year 5
© A & C Black

Do the splits

• **Split the numbers to show the value of each digit.**

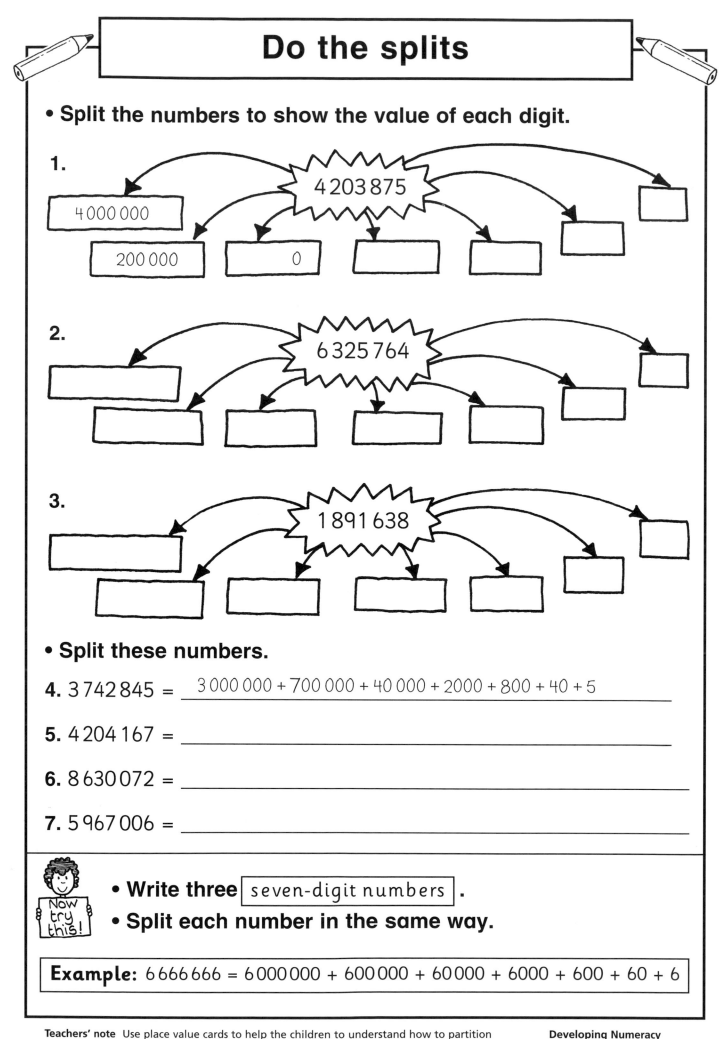

1.

4 203 875

4 000 000   200 000   0

2.

6 325 764

3.

1 891 638

• **Split these numbers.**

4. 3 742 845 = 3 000 000 + 700 000 + 40 000 + 2000 + 800 + 40 + 5

5. 4 204 167 = _____

6. 8 630 072 = _____

7. 5 967 006 = _____

• **Write three** | seven-digit numbers | .

• **Split each number in the same way.**

Example: 6 666 666 = 6 000 000 + 600 000 + 60 000 + 6000 + 600 + 60 + 6

Teachers' note Use place value cards to help the children to understand how to partition numbers.

Developing Numeracy
Numbers and the Number System
Year 5
© A & C Black

The maths marvel multiples

The maths marvel says:

When you multiply a number by 10, the digits move <u>one</u> place to the left.

When you multiply a number by 100, the digits move <u>two</u> places to the left.

• **Use these columns to multiply numbers by** 10 **or by** 100 **.**

	TTh	Th	H	T	U			HTh	TTh	Th	H	T	U
1.					6	x 10 =						6	0
2.				1	4	x 10 =							
3.			3	6	1	x 10 =							
4.	5	2	7	1	3	x 10 =							
5.				2	8	x 100 =							
6.			1	0	4	x 100 =							
7.			2	6	0	x 100 =							
8.				0	0	x 100 =							

• **How many times larger is the first number than the second?**

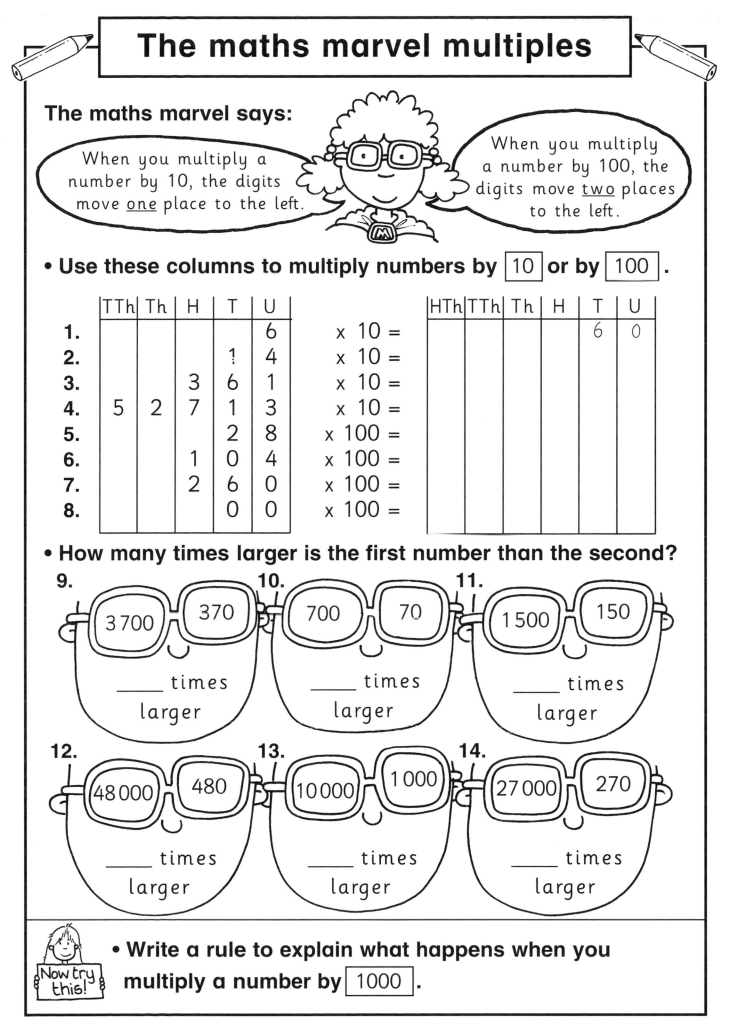

9. 3 700   370
_____ times larger

10. 700   70
_____ times larger

11. 1 500   150
_____ times larger

12. 48 000   480
_____ times larger

13. 10 000   1 000
_____ times larger

14. 27 000   270
_____ times larger

Now try this!

• **Write a rule to explain what happens when you multiply a number by** 1000 **.**

Teachers' note Discuss the effect of multiplying decimals by 10, for example, 3·4, 8·21.

Developing Numeracy
Numbers and the Number System
Year 5
© A & C Black

13

The maths marvel divides

The maths marvel says:

When you divide a number by 10, the digits move <u>one</u> place to the right.

When you divide a number by 100, the digits move <u>two</u> places to the right.

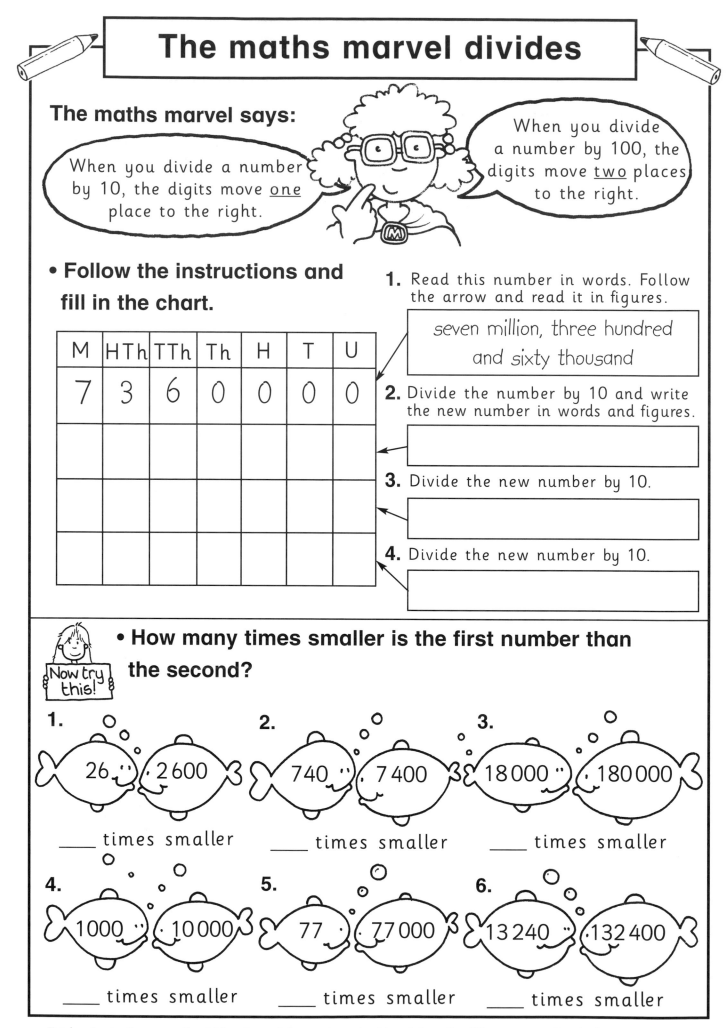

• **Follow the instructions and fill in the chart.**

M	HTh	TTh	Th	H	T	U
7	3	6	0	0	0	0

1. Read this number in words. Follow the arrow and read it in figures.

   seven million, three hundred and sixty thousand

2. Divide the number by 10 and write the new number in words and figures.

3. Divide the new number by 10.

4. Divide the new number by 10.

• **How many times smaller is the first number than the second?**

1. 26 · 2600

_____ times smaller

2. 740 · 7400

_____ times smaller

3. 18 000 · 180 000

_____ times smaller

4. 1000 · 10 000

_____ times smaller

5. 77 · 77 000

_____ times smaller

6. 13 240 · 132 400

_____ times smaller

Teachers' note Encourage the children to read the numbers aloud to reinforce the different values of a digit in the different positions.

Developing Numeracy
Numbers and the Number System
Year 5
© A & C Black

14

More or less?

• **Circle the larger number in each pair.**

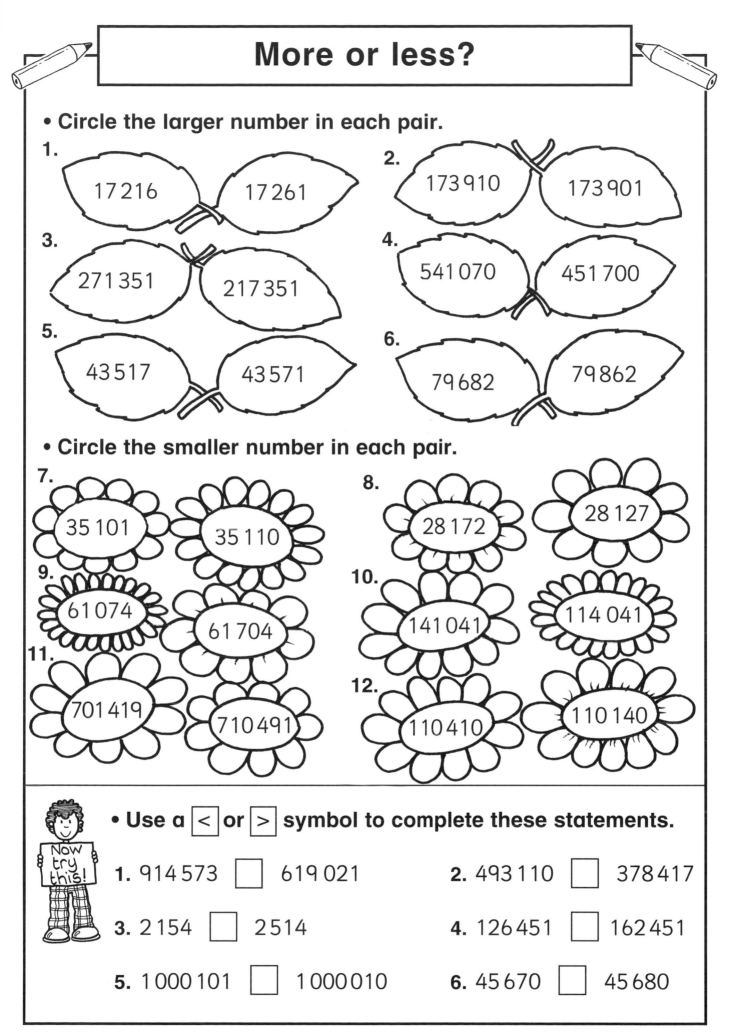

1. 17 216   17 261

2. 173 910   173 901

3. 271 351   217 351

4. 541 070   451 700

5. 43 517   43 571

6. 79 682   79 862

• **Circle the smaller number in each pair.**

7. 35 101   35 110

8. 28 172   28 127

9. 61 074   61 704

10. 141 041   114 041

11. 701 419   710 491

12. 110 410   110 140

• **Use a** $<$ **or** $>$ **symbol to complete these statements.**

Now try this!

1. 914 573 ☐ 619 021

2. 493 110 ☐ 378 417

3. 2 154 ☐ 2 514

4. 126 451 ☐ 162 451

5. 1 000 101 ☐ 1 000 010

6. 45 670 ☐ 45 680

Teachers' note A useful way to describe the 'greater than' and 'less than' signs is as a hungry crocodile's mouth which is always open towards the larger number.

Developing Numeracy
Numbers and the Number System
Year 5
© A & C Black

In the right order

- **Write the numbers in ascending order on the skipping ropes.**

1.
692   725

| 9 543 | 5 617 | 1 899 | 6 820 | ~~692~~ | ~~725~~ |

2.

| 23 645 | 25 499 | 2 847 | 29 110 | 2 562 | 294 |

3.

| 4 512 | 3 619 | 4 160 | 4 261 | 4 159 | 589 |

- **Write, in order, two numbers that lie between each pair.**

4. 89 735 _____ _____ 95 701
5. 171 907 _____ _____ 199 999
6. 347 656 _____ _____ 348 912
7. 484 713 _____ _____ 485 212
8. 971 598 _____ _____ 971 601
9. 699 999 _____ _____ 700 002

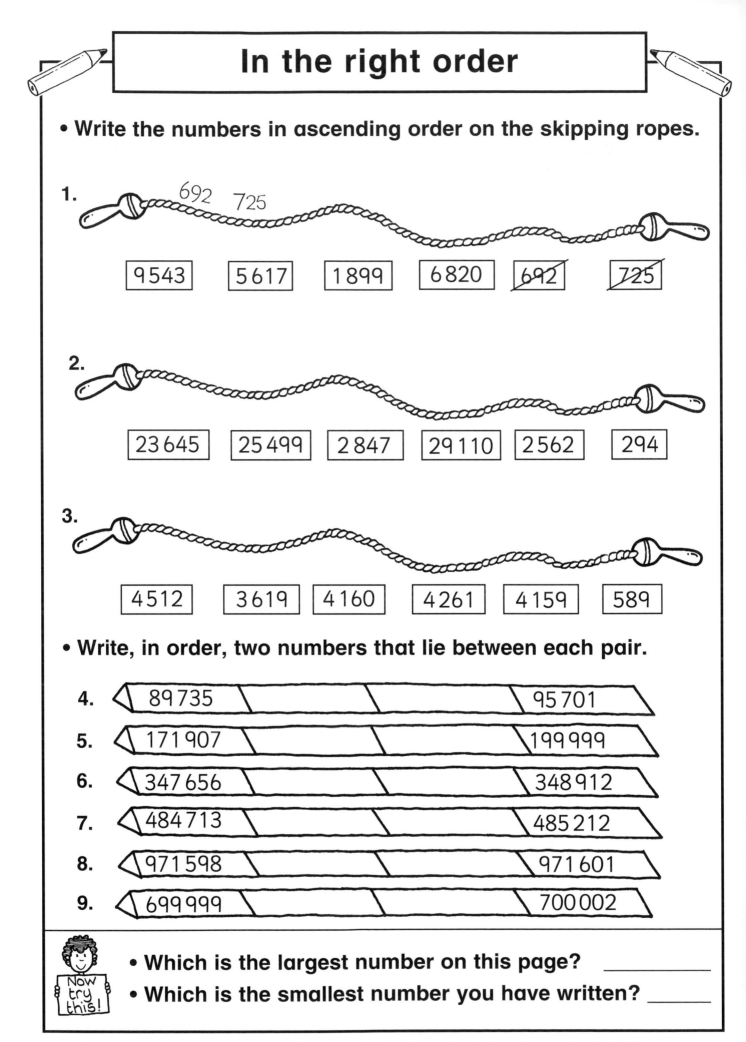

Now try this!

- **Which is the largest number on this page?** _____
- **Which is the smallest number you have written?** _____

Teachers' note Children may need further reinforcement of their understanding of place value, particularly if they are writing commas in inappropriate places in larger numbers, such as 1,42,30.

**Developing Numeracy
Numbers and the Number System
Year 5
© A & C Black**

Target practice

- Use the digits $\boxed{2}$, $\boxed{4}$, $\boxed{5}$ and $\boxed{0}$ in each question. The answer that they make should be as close as possible to the target number.

1. $\boxed{2}\ \boxed{4} + \boxed{5}\ \boxed{0} = $ **74**

2. $\boxed{}\ \boxed{}\ \boxed{} \times \boxed{} = $ **900**

3. $\boxed{}\ \boxed{} \times \boxed{}\ \boxed{} = $ **110**

4. $\boxed{}\ \boxed{}\ \boxed{} + \boxed{} = $ **210**

5. $\boxed{}\ \boxed{}\ \boxed{} - \boxed{} = $ **425**

6. $\boxed{}\ \boxed{}\ \boxed{} \div \boxed{} = $ **80**

Use all the digits each time.

Now try this!

- Now use the digits $\boxed{1}$, $\boxed{3}$, $\boxed{5}$ and $\boxed{2}$.
- How close can you get to the same target numbers?

Example: $51 + 73 = 74$

Teachers' note Provide digit cards for the numbers on this page and allow the children to rearrange them as necessary. You might want to point out that the children will need to use zero as a place holder in question 3.

**Developing Numeracy
Numbers and the Number System
Year 5
© A & C Black**

How many do you think?

- Estimate the number of bricks in these walls.

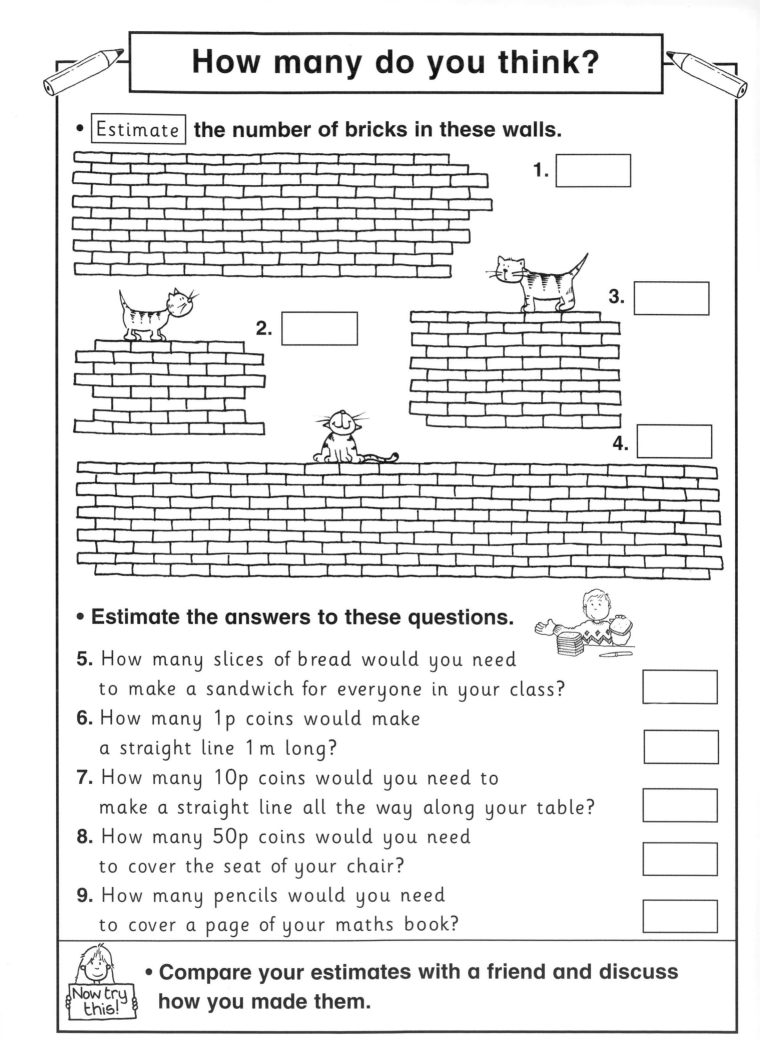

1. ☐

2. ☐

3. ☐

4. ☐

- **Estimate the answers to these questions.**

5. How many slices of bread would you need to make a sandwich for everyone in your class? ☐

6. How many 1p coins would make a straight line 1 m long? ☐

7. How many 10p coins would you need to make a straight line all the way along your table? ☐

8. How many 50p coins would you need to cover the seat of your chair? ☐

9. How many pencils would you need to cover a page of your maths book? ☐

Now try this!

- **Compare your estimates with a friend and discuss how you made them.**

Teachers' note In the first activity, encourage the children to count the number of bricks in one row of the wall and then to use multiplication. For the first question in the second activity, suggest to the children that two pieces of bread would be used to make each sandwich.

Developing Numeracy
Numbers and the Number System
Year 5
© A & C Black

18

Where's the arrow?

- Estimate the position of each arrow on the number lines.

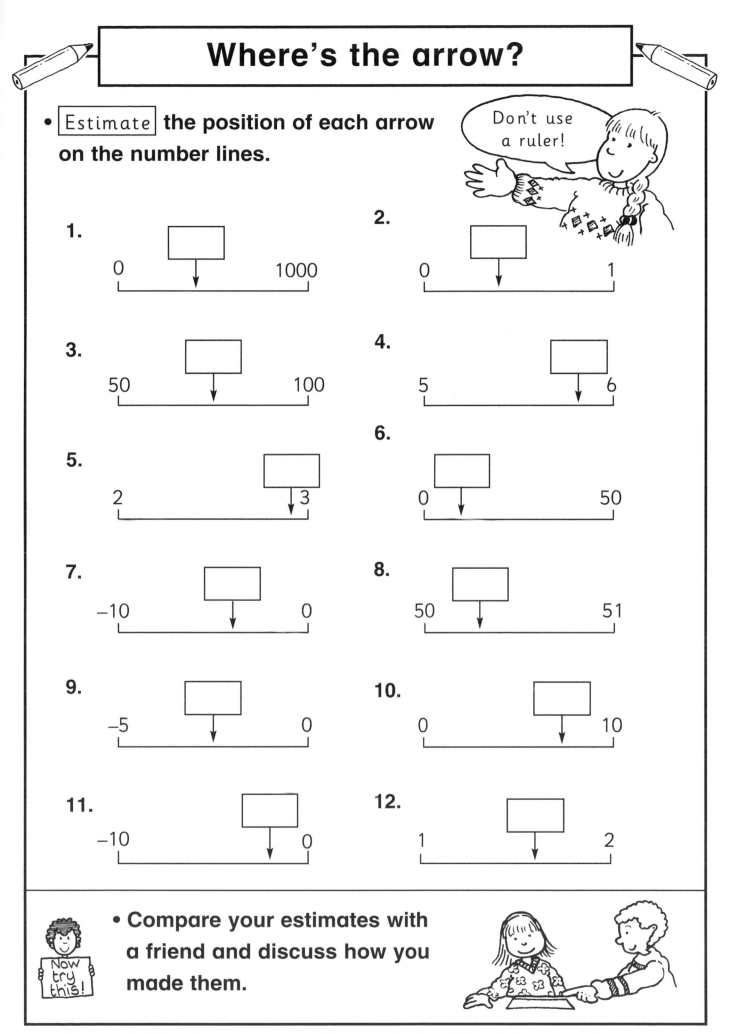

Don't use a ruler!

1.
0   1000

2.
0   1

3.
50   100

4.
5   6

5.
2   3

6.
0   50

7.
−10   0

8.
50   51

9.
−5   0

10.
0   10

11.
−10   0

12.
1   2

Now try this!

- Compare your estimates with a friend and discuss how you made them.

Teachers' note The children should practise working with empty number lines of this type before they tackle this activity.

Developing Numeracy
Numbers and the Number System
Year 5
© A & C Black

19

Goal!

- **Round the numbers on the footballs to the** $\boxed{\text{nearest 10}}$.
- **Draw a line from each ball to the correct goal.**

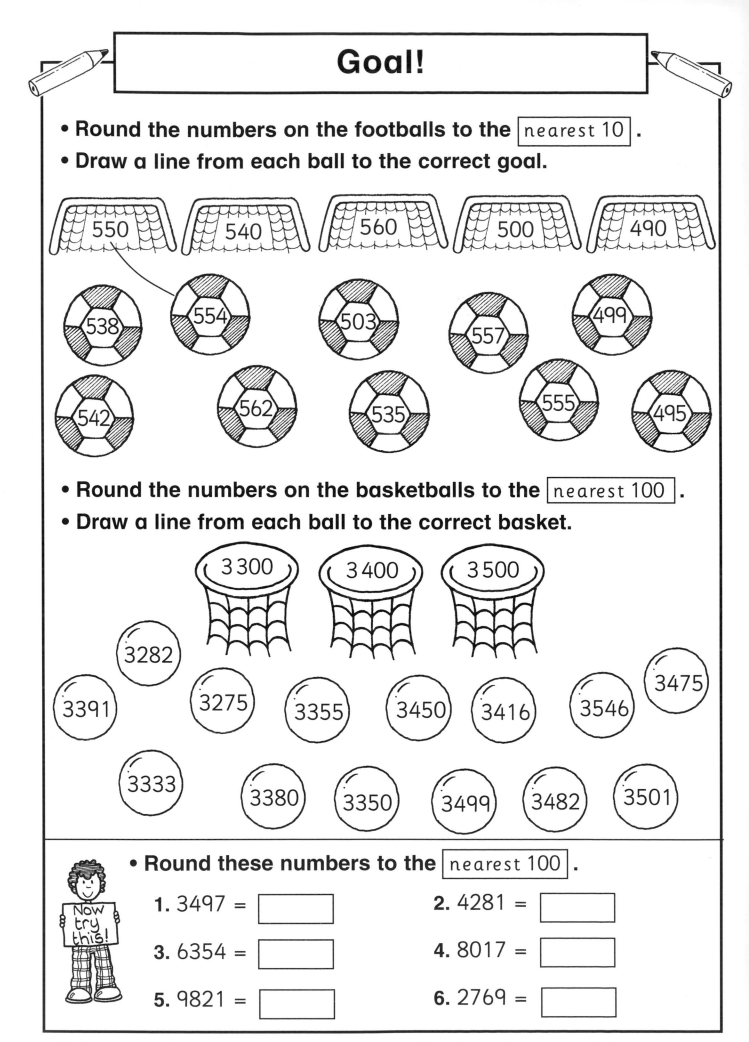

| 550 | 540 | 560 | 500 | 490 |

538   554   503   557   499

542   562   535   555   495

- **Round the numbers on the basketballs to the** $\boxed{\text{nearest 100}}$.
- **Draw a line from each ball to the correct basket.**

| 3 300 | 3 400 | 3 500 |

3282   3391   3275   3355   3450   3416   3546   3475

3333   3380   3350   3499   3482   3501

- **Round these numbers to the** $\boxed{\text{nearest 100}}$.

1. 3497 = ☐ **2.** 4281 = ☐

3. 6354 = ☐ **4.** 8017 = ☐

5. 9821 = ☐ **6.** 2769 = ☐

Teachers' note Remind the children that a number with five units usually rounds up to the nearest ten. Suggest to the children that they use a different colour to draw the lines to each goal or basket. As a further extension activity, ask the children to write down the smallest and largest number that will round to one of the numbers in the baskets (to the nearest 100).

Developing Numeracy
Numbers and the Number System
Year 5
© A & C Black

Earth facts

- **Here are the heights of some volcanoes.**
  Round them to the nearest
  10 m , 100 m **and** 1000 m .

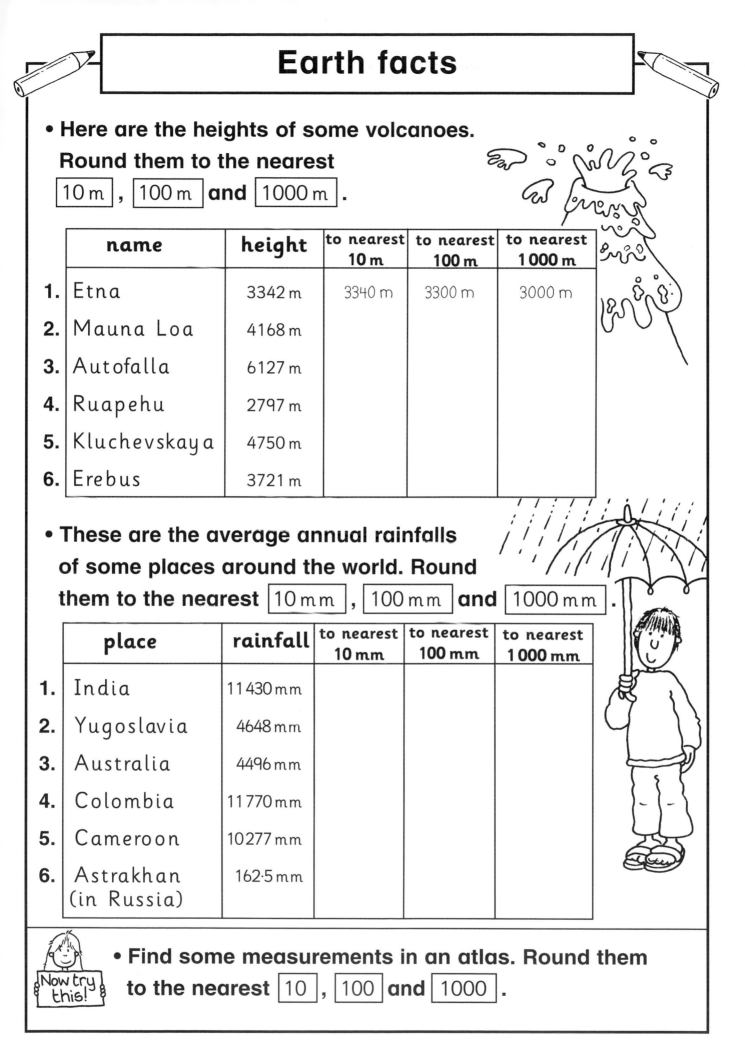

	name	height	to nearest 10 m	to nearest 100 m	to nearest 1000 m
1.	Etna	3342 m	3340 m	3300 m	3000 m
2.	Mauna Loa	4168 m			
3.	Autofalla	6127 m			
4.	Ruapehu	2797 m			
5.	Kluchevskaya	4750 m			
6.	Erebus	3721 m			

- **These are the average annual rainfalls
  of some places around the world. Round
  them to the nearest** 10 mm , 100 mm **and** 1000 mm .

	place	rainfall	to nearest 10 mm	to nearest 100 mm	to nearest 1000 mm
1.	India	11430 mm			
2.	Yugoslavia	4648 mm			
3.	Australia	4496 mm			
4.	Colombia	11770 mm			
5.	Cameroon	10277 mm			
6.	Astrakhan (in Russia)	162·5 mm			

Now try this!

- **Find some measurements in an atlas. Round them
  to the nearest** 10 , 100 **and** 1000 .

Teachers' note Remind children that 5, 50 and 500 will round up to the nearest 10, 100, 1000 respectively. They should include the unit of measurement in their answers.

**Developing Numeracy
Numbers and the Number System
Year 5
© A & C Black**

21

Below zero

• **Complete this number track.**

									−1	0	1	2

• **Write the number that is**

1. 2 less than 0 ☐   **2.** 4 less than −2 ☐

3. 5 less than 1 ☐   **4.** 7 less than 2 ☐

5. 9 less than 1 ☐   **6.** 5 less than −1 ☐

• **Write the missing numbers.**

7. −6 < ☐ < −4   **8.** −1 < ☐ < 1

9. −8 < ☐ < ☐ < −5   **10.** −2 < ☐ < ☐ < 1

• **Continue the pattern on each snake.**

11.

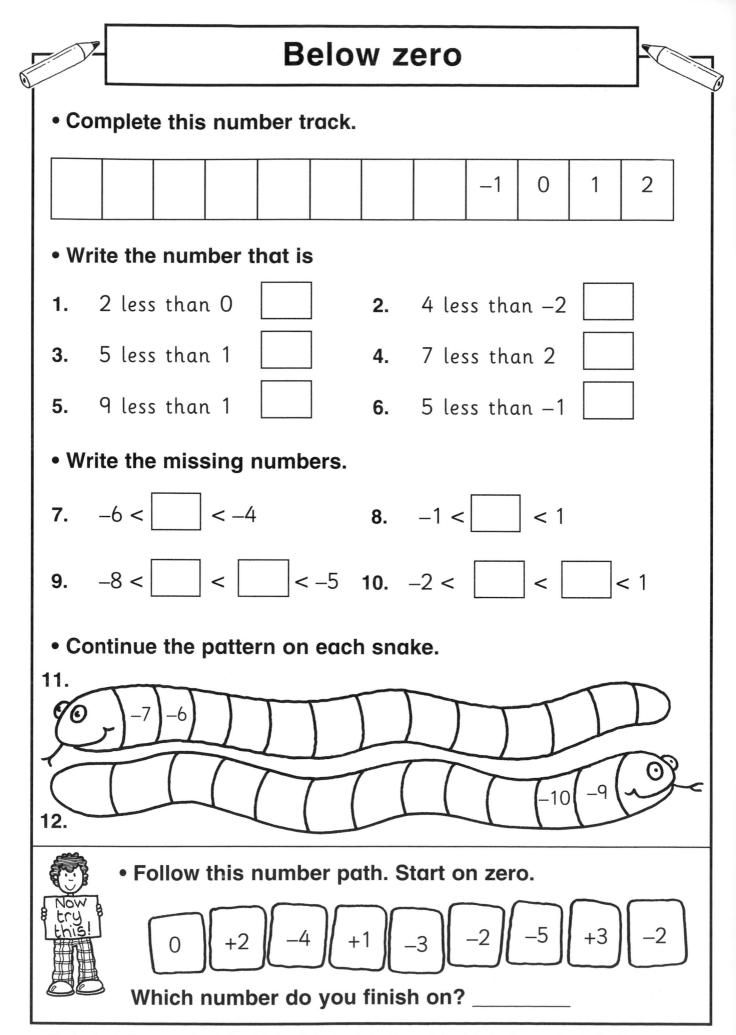

−7 −6

−10 −9

12.

• **Follow this number path. Start on zero.**

Now try this!

| 0 | +2 | −4 | +1 | −3 | −2 | −5 | +3 | −2 |

Which number do you finish on? _____

Teachers' note Practise number chains with the whole class during the mental/oral starter. As a further extension, the children could write number paths for their friends to follow and find the final number. Ensure that they first work out the answers for themselves.

Developing Numeracy
Numbers and the Number System
Year 5
© A & C Black

Weather watch

• **Fill in the gaps on the chart. Use the thermometer to help you.**

°C –14 –13 –12 –11 –10 –9 –8 –7 –6 –5 –4 –3 –2 –1 0 1 2 3 4 5 6 7 8 9 10

	Yesterday's temperature	Temperature change	Today's temperature
1.	3°C	rose by 2°C	5°C
2.	1°C	dropped by 3°C	___
3.	–5°C	increased by 1°C	___
4.	–7°C	decreased by 2°C	___
5.	–1°C	rose by 2°C	___
6.	1°C	dropped by 9°C	___
7.	2°C	decreased by 10°C	___
8.	–6°C	increased by 10°C	–4°C
9.	___	fell by 3°C	2°C
10.	___	rose by 8°C	0°C
11.	___	decreased by 10°C	9°C
12.	___	increased by 19°C	

This chart shows the temperature in five capital cities.

London	0°C
Paris	3°C
Bonn	5°C
Moscow	–14°C
Washington	–2°C

• **Write the difference in temperature between**

1. Paris and London _____

2. Bonn and Moscow _____

3. Washington and Paris _____

4. Moscow and London _____

Teachers' note Encourage the children to use the number sequence on the thermometer to check their answers.

Developing Numeracy
Numbers and the Number System
Year 5
© A & C Black

23

Forwards and backwards

- **Continue these patterns.**

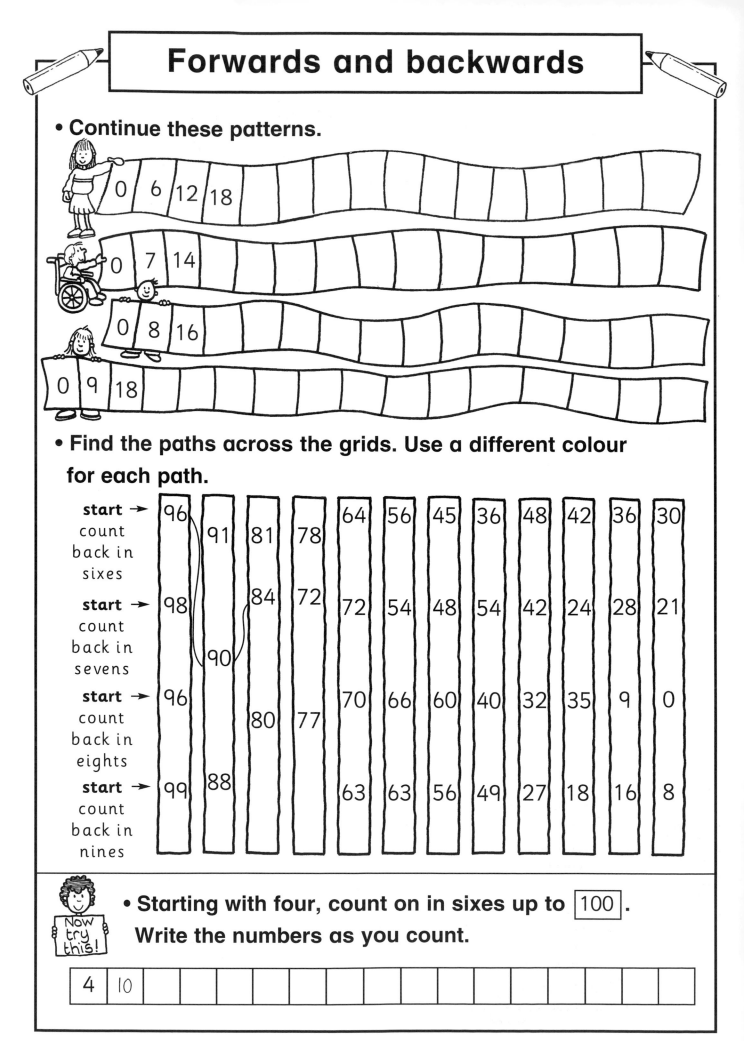

0 | 6 | 12 | 18

0 | 7 | 14

0 | 8 | 16

0 | 9 | 18

- **Find the paths across the grids. Use a different colour for each path.**

start → count back in sixes
96 | 91 | 81 | 78 | 64 | 56 | 45 | 36 | 48 | 42 | 36 | 30

start → count back in sevens
98 | | 84 | 72 | 72 | 54 | 48 | 54 | 42 | 24 | 28 | 21
| | 90

start → count back in eights
96 | | | | 70 | 66 | 60 | 40 | 32 | 35 | 9 | 0
| | 80 | 77

start → count back in nines
99 | 88 | | | 63 | 63 | 56 | 49 | 27 | 18 | 16 | 8

- **Starting with four, count on in sixes up to** 100 .
  Write the numbers as you count.

4 | 10 | | | | | | | | | | | | | | |

Teachers' note The children may notice that, when counting from zero in different-sized steps, some multiples of one number are also multiples of another.

Developing Numeracy
Numbers and the Number System
Year 5
© A & C Black

Find the pattern

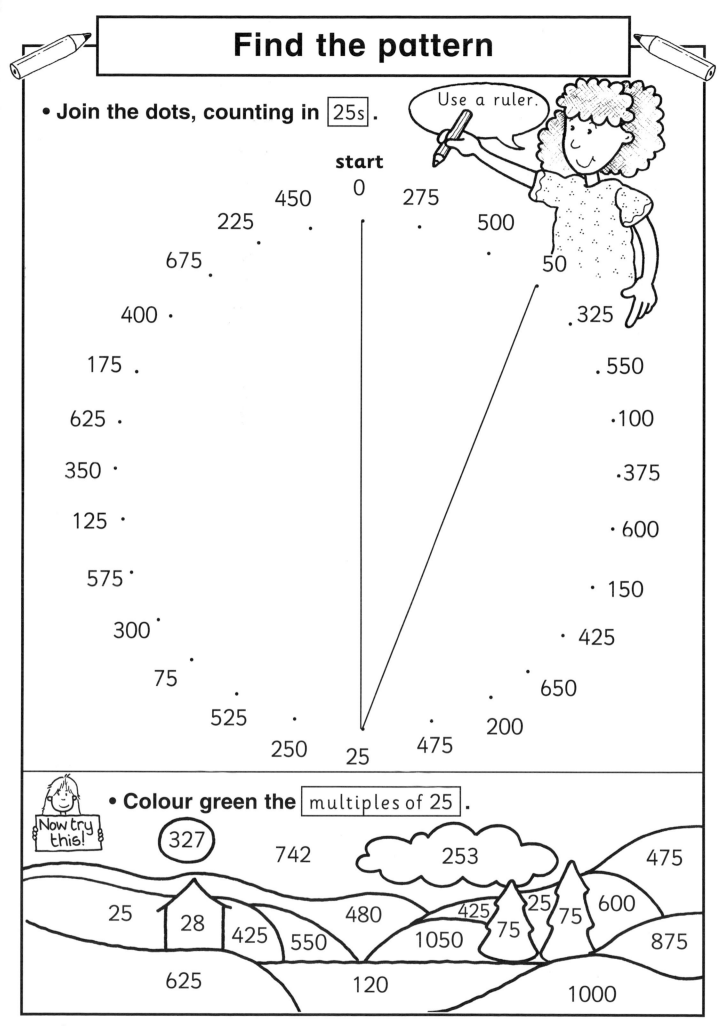

• **Join the dots, counting in** 25s .

Use a ruler.

start

0

450   275

225   500

675   50

400   . 325

175   . 550

625   . 100

350   . 375

125   . 600

575   . 150

300   . 425

75   650

525   . 200

250   25   475

• **Colour green the** multiples of 25 .

Now try this!

327

742   253   475

25   28   425   480   425 25 75 600

550   1050   75   875

625   120   1000

Teachers' note Demonstrate to the children the link between counting in 25s and counting in 2·5s or 250s.

Developing Numeracy
Numbers and the Number System
Year 5
© A & C Black

25

Number maze

• **Follow the path through the maze. Can you reach the finish?**

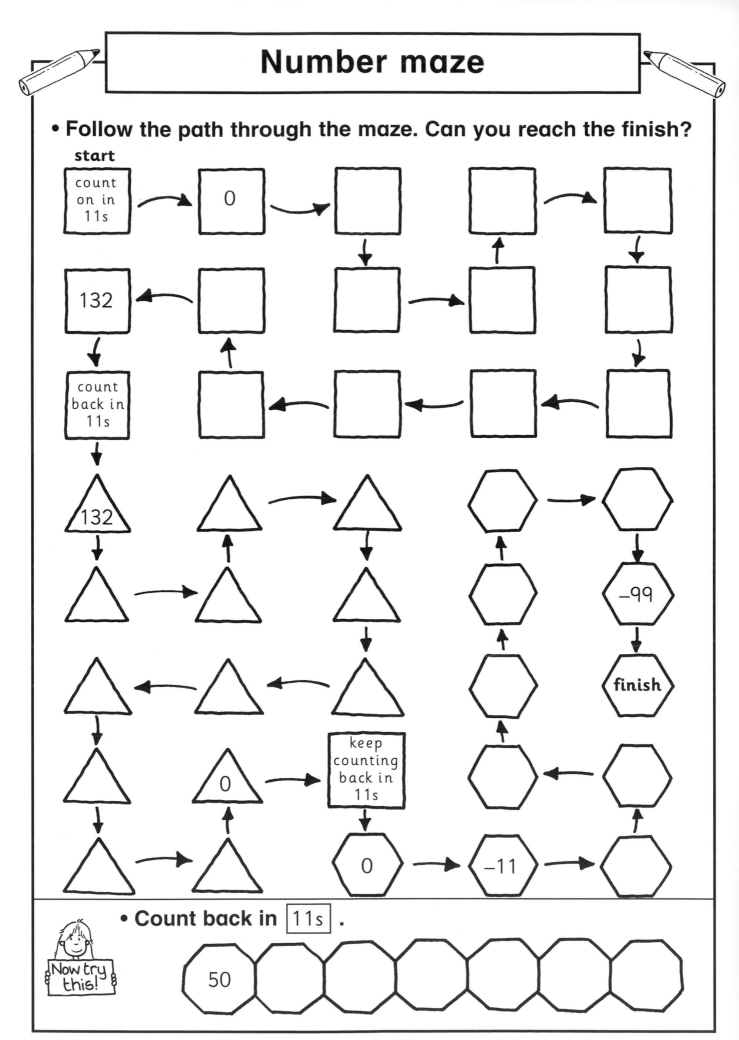

start

count on in 11s → 0 → ☐ → ☐ → ☐

132 ← ☐ ☐ → ☐ ☐

count back in 11s ☐ ☐ ☐ ☐

132 △ △ ◯ → ◯

△ △ △ ◯ -99

△ ← △ ← △ ◯ finish

△ keep counting back in 11s ◯ ◯

△ → 0 → ◯ 0 → -11 → ◯

• **Count back in** 11s .

50 ◯ ◯ ◯ ◯ ◯ ◯

Now try this!

Teachers' note The numbers in the maze can be masked before photocopying to provide a flexible resource.

Developing Numeracy
Numbers and the Number System
Year 5
© A & C Black

Counting cards

- **Cut out the cards and put them in a pile face down.**
- **Take turns to pick a card and count aloud.**
- **Write down the numbers.**

Ask a friend to check your answers.

1. Count on from 24 to 96 in steps of 8 .	**2.** Count on from 35 to 98 in steps of 7 .	**3.** Count back from 99 to 0 in steps of 9 .
4. Count back from 475 to 300 in steps of 25 .	**5.** Count on from 24 to 96 in steps of 6 .	**6.** Count back from 88 to 0 in steps of 8 .
7. Count on from 0 to 225 in steps of 25 .	**8.** Count on from 0 to 2 in steps of 0·1 .	**9.** Count back from 4·8 to 3·2 in steps of 0·1 .
10. Count back from 99 to 0 in steps of 11 .	**11.** Count on from 0 to 132 in steps of 11 .	**12.** Count back from 0 to −88 in steps of 11 .
13. Count on from 2·8 to 4·6 in steps of 0·1 .	**14.** Count back from 84 to 0 in steps of 7 .	**15.** Count on from 88 to 132 in steps of 11 .
16. Count on from 1 to 111 in steps of 11 .	**17.** Count back from 1000 to 250 in steps of 250 .	**18.** Count on from −33 to 55 in steps of 11 .

Teachers' note This game also makes a good mental/oral starter activity for the whole class.

Developing Numeracy
Numbers and the Number System
Year 5
© A & C Black

Count in eights

zero

1	2	3	4	5	6	7	8
9	10	11	12	13	14	15	16
17	18	19	20	21	22	23	24
25	26	27	28	29	30	31	32
33	34	35	36	37	38	39	40
41	42	43	44	45	46	47	48
49	50	51	52	53	54	55	56
57	58	59	60	61	62	63	64

- **Count on from zero in** eights **. Colour the numbers blue.**

- **Count on from zero in** fours **. Colour the numbers yellow.**

- **What do you notice?** _____

_____

- **Count on from zero in** sevens **. Colour the numbers orange.
  Which numbers are already coloured?** _____

- **Count on from zero in** threes **. Circle the numbers.
  What do you notice?** _____

_____

Now try this!

- **Draw a 7 x 7 number grid.**
- **Count on from zero in** sixes **and** threes **.**
- **Colour the numbers. What do you notice?**

Teachers' note Encourage the children to explore patterns of multiples on different-sized grids.

**Developing Numeracy
Numbers and the Number System
Year 5
© A & C Black**

28

Odds and evens

• **Fill in the answers.**

1. 7 + 5 + 3 =

2. 15 − 7 =

4. 5 + 11 + 7 =

3. 8 + 12 + 22 =

5. 24 − 7 =

6. 4 + 36 + 20 =

8. 32 − 16 =

7. 27 − 9 =

• **Write** odd **or** even **in each cloud.**

9. even + even + even =

10. odd + odd + odd =

11. even − odd =

12. even − even =

13. odd − even =

14. odd − odd =

Use the questions above to help you.

Now try this!

• **Make up two examples to test each** odd **and** even **statement.**

Teachers' note Encourage the children to appreciate that they need to provide more than one example to prove a general statement.

**Developing Numeracy
Numbers and the Number System
Year 5
© A & C Black**

29

Multiple mystery tour

- **Choose a bus.**
- **Follow the road numbers which are multiples of the number on your bus.**
- **Where does the bus take you?**
- **Now do the same with the other buses.**

Write the bus number on the place where it ends up.

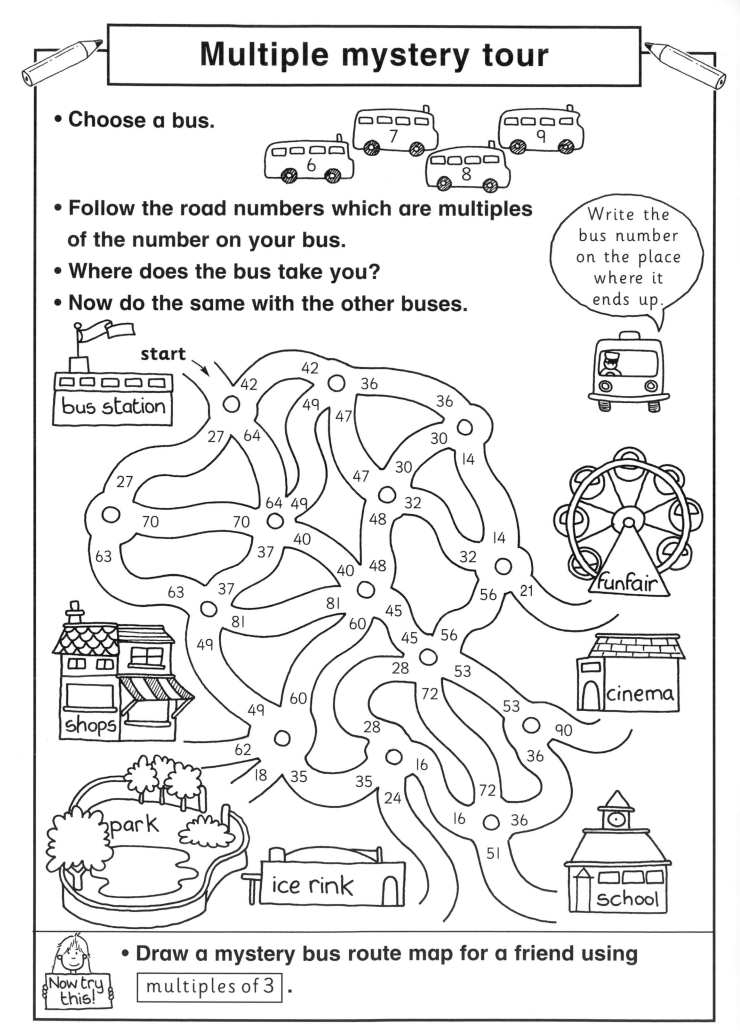

- **Draw a mystery bus route map for a friend using** multiples of 3 .

Teachers' note Children may discover that some numbers are common multiples, i.e. that they are multiples of more than one number.

Developing Numeracy
Numbers and the Number System
Year 5
© A & C Black

The multiple game

| 6 | 7 | 8 | 9 |

- Cut out the cards above and put them face down.
- Take turns to pick a card. Put a counter on one multiple of the number on your card. Put the card back.
- The winner is the first to have four counters in a line, vertically, horizontally or diagonally.

18	63	81	48	32	54	36
54	42	24	56	45	64	21
30	27	40	72	24	42	81
28	35	64	48	80	36	72
72	54	56	48	63	70	49
60	36	42	49	21	56	90

Teachers' note This game can be played by two or three players. Each player needs a different coloured set of counters. Children will discover that many numbers are common multiples.

**Developing Numeracy
Numbers and the Number System
Year 5
© A & C Black**

31

Sort the numbers

- **Look closely at the numbers in this Venn diagram.**
- **Complete the labels for each circle.**

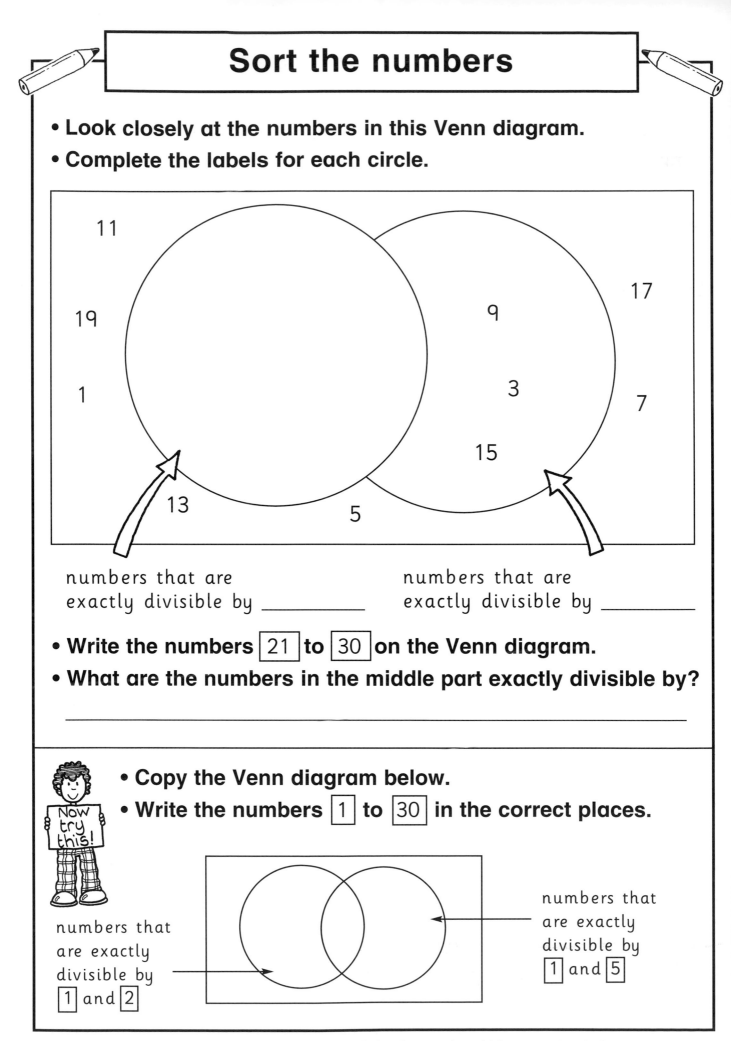

11

19

1

13

9

3

15

5

17

7

numbers that are
exactly divisible by _____

numbers that are
exactly divisible by _____

- **Write the numbers 21 to 30 on the Venn diagram.**
- **What are the numbers in the middle part exactly divisible by?**

_____

- **Copy the Venn diagram below.**
- **Write the numbers 1 to 30 in the correct places.**

Now try this!

numbers that
are exactly
divisible by
1 and 2

numbers that
are exactly
divisible by
1 and 5

Teachers' note Encourage the children to use a range of vocabulary, for example, multiple, exactly divisible by and so on. You may wish to remind the children that the numbers in the Venn diagram can be divisible by more than one number. In the extension activity, point out to the children that the Venn diagram will need to be about four times the size of the one shown here.

Developing Numeracy
Numbers and the Number System
Year 5
© **A & C Black**

Division puzzle

- **There is a letter hidden in each grid.**
- **To find the letters, colour the numbers that are:**

exactly divisible by 5

1.

300	47	341
5	82	86
175	303	22
35	172	144
85	90	910

2.

410	100	50
45	72	375
875	80	25
60	43	70
125	49	380

exactly divisible by 10

3.

230	50	47
100	85	30
180	105	600
70	27	110
80	900	83

4.

170	63	360
180	103	300
701	6000	49
65	40	142
166	90	144

exactly divisible by 100

5.

2000	300	8300
100	20	2400
1000	1600	60
400	40	600
800	6300	3400

6.

200	1500	1100
87	900	606
360	300	873
40	6400	901
3500	6000	8000

exactly divisible by 4

7.

36	148	40
80	71	216
320	400	12
16	160	23
24	141	48

8.

364	612	123
340	131	132
144	22	316
248	350	220
640	124	645

- **What word do the letters make?** _____

Teachers' note As the extension to the activity on this page, ask the children to write rules to explain how they can recognise the multiples of 2, 4, 5, 10 and 100.

**Developing Numeracy
Numbers and the Number System
Year 5
© A & C Black**

Square number snap

- **Cut out the cards, mix them up and deal them out evenly with a friend.**
- **Play 'square number snap'!**

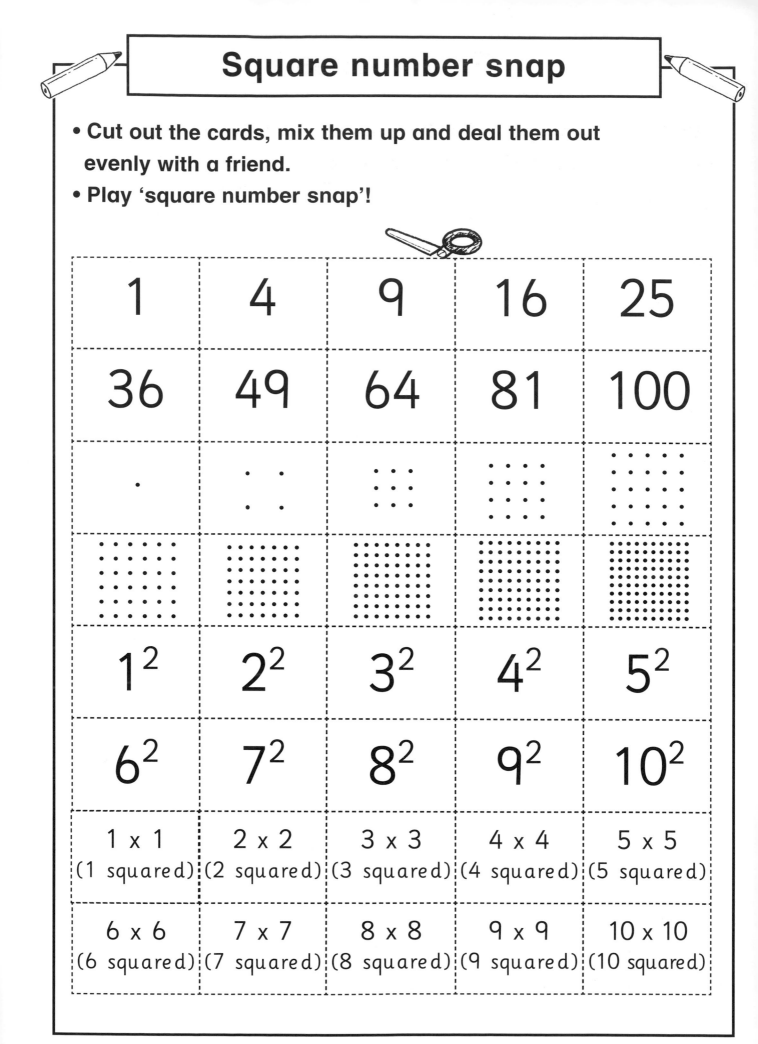

Teachers' note Photocopy this page on to A3 card for each pair of children. Draw the children's attention to square numbers on a multiplication tables square.

**Developing Numeracy
Numbers and the Number System
Year 5
© A & C Black**

Factor trees

- Write the factor pairs for the number on each tree trunk.
- Use a different leaf for each factor pair.

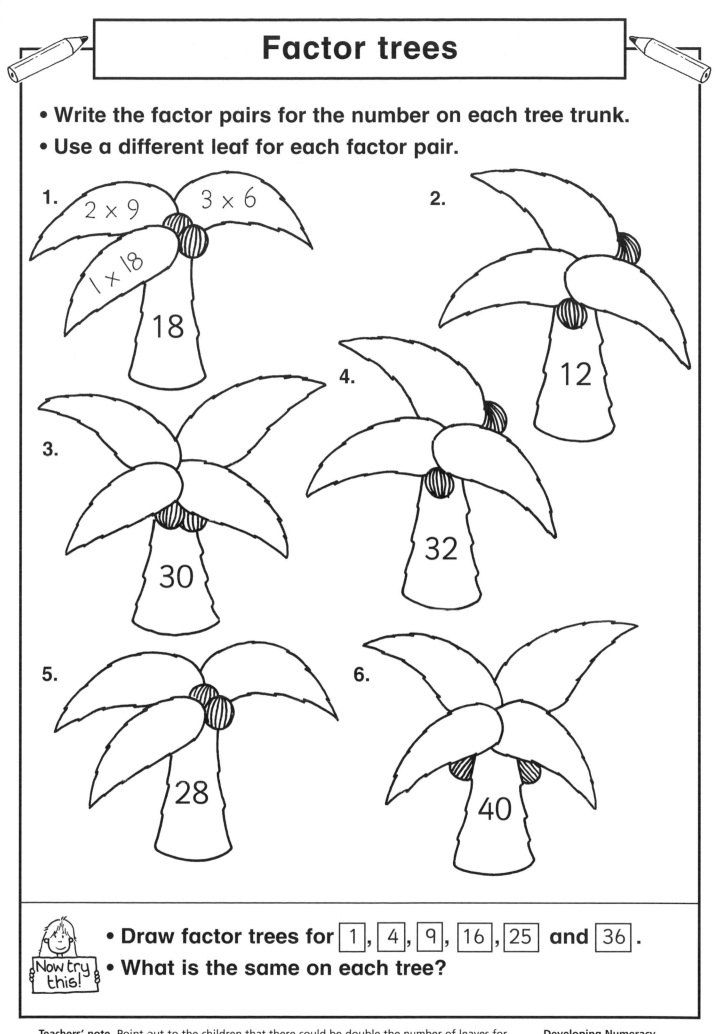

1. 2×9 3×6 1×18 — 18

2. 12

3. 30

4. 32

5. 28

6. 40

- Draw factor trees for 1 , 4 , 9 , 16 , 25 and 36 .
- What is the same on each tree?

Teachers' note Point out to the children that there could be double the number of leaves for each tree with the factors reversed. As an additional extension activity the children could continue factor trees for other square numbers.

Developing Numeracy
Numbers and the Number System
Year 5
© A & C Black

Factor wheels

• **Write in each carriage a different factor for the number in the middle.**

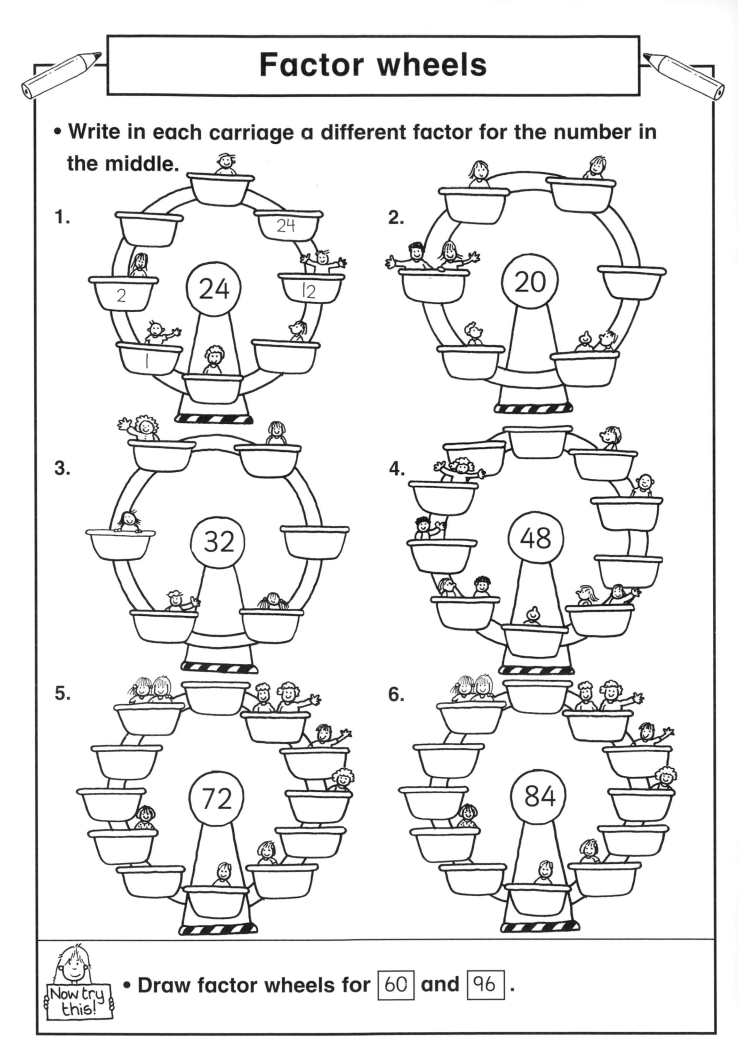

1. 24 — 24, 2, 12, 1

2. 20

3. 32

4. 48

5. 72

6. 84

Now try this!

• **Draw factor wheels for** 60 **and** 96 .

Teachers' note Children can draw factor wheels for other numbers to 100. It may help the children to write in opposite carriages the factors that multiply together to make the central number.

**Developing Numeracy
Numbers and the Number System
Year 5
© A & C Black**

Fraction boards

- Write these fractions on the correct boards. Some fractions belong on more than one board.

$\frac{1}{3}$ $\frac{4}{7}$ $\frac{6}{8}$ $1\frac{9}{5}$ $\frac{14}{8}$ $5\frac{4}{9}$

$6\frac{7}{14}$ $\frac{7}{10}$ $2\frac{4}{5}$ $\frac{1}{9}$ $\frac{15}{10}$ $3\frac{7}{8}$ $\frac{1}{10}$

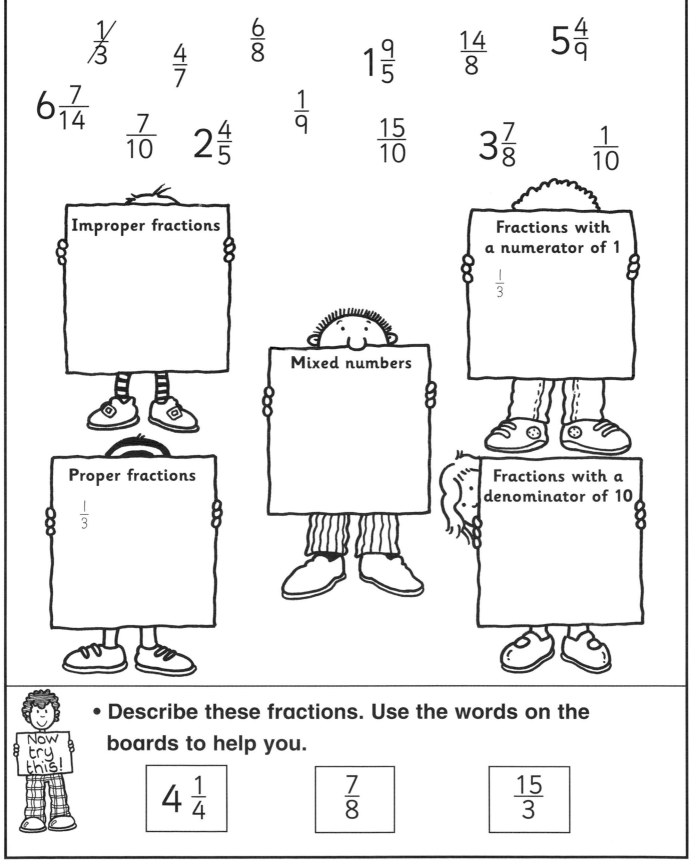

Improper fractions

Mixed numbers

Fractions with a numerator of 1
$\frac{1}{3}$

Proper fractions
$\frac{1}{3}$

Fractions with a denominator of 10

- Describe these fractions. Use the words on the boards to help you.

$4\frac{1}{4}$ $\frac{7}{8}$ $\frac{15}{3}$

Teachers' note It is important that the children are familiar with the terms on this page and that they use them to describe different fractions. As a further extension activity, they could write definitions for the terms.

**Developing Numeracy
Numbers and the Number System
Year 5**
© A & C Black

Catch the kite

• **Join the improper fractions to their** equivalent **mixed numbers.**

1. $\frac{5}{2}$

2. $\frac{12}{10}$

3. $\frac{7}{4}$

4. $\frac{11}{5}$

5. $\frac{25}{4}$

6. $\frac{17}{4}$

7. $\frac{32}{10}$

8. $\frac{41}{10}$

9. $\frac{7}{2}$

$1\frac{2}{10}$ $2\frac{1}{2}$ $4\frac{1}{10}$ $3\frac{1}{2}$

$2\frac{1}{5}$ $3\frac{2}{10}$ $1\frac{3}{4}$ $6\frac{1}{4}$ $4\frac{1}{4}$

• **Write the equivalent fractions and mixed numbers.**

Now try this!

1. $2\frac{1}{4}$

2. $\frac{43}{10}$

3. $6\frac{2}{10}$

4. $\frac{12}{5}$

5. $7\frac{3}{5}$

6. $\frac{42}{4}$

Teachers' note Provide a visual representation of mixed numbers, for example, cakes or pizzas to help the children to understand them.

Developing Numeracy
Numbers and the Number System
Year 5
© A & C Black

True or false?

• **Colour the banners that are true.**

1. Half of one sixth is one third.

2. One quarter is half of a half.

3. Half of a quarter is one half.

4. Halve one tenth to find one fifth.

5. Half of one third is one sixth.

6. Half of one eighth is a quarter.

7. One tenth is half a twentieth.

8. Half of one quarter is one eighth.

9. One twentieth is half of one tenth.

10. Half of one fifth is one tenth.

• **Start with one whole, and follow these instructions:**

| Find half. | Now halve that. | Halve it once more! |

What fraction are you left with?

Teachers' note Provide the children with fraction boards or fraction circles to check their answers.

**Developing Numeracy
Numbers and the Number System
Year 5
© A & C Black**

Fraction teams

- Sort the children into two teams. In each team the fractions should be equivalent .
- Write the fractions in the circles.

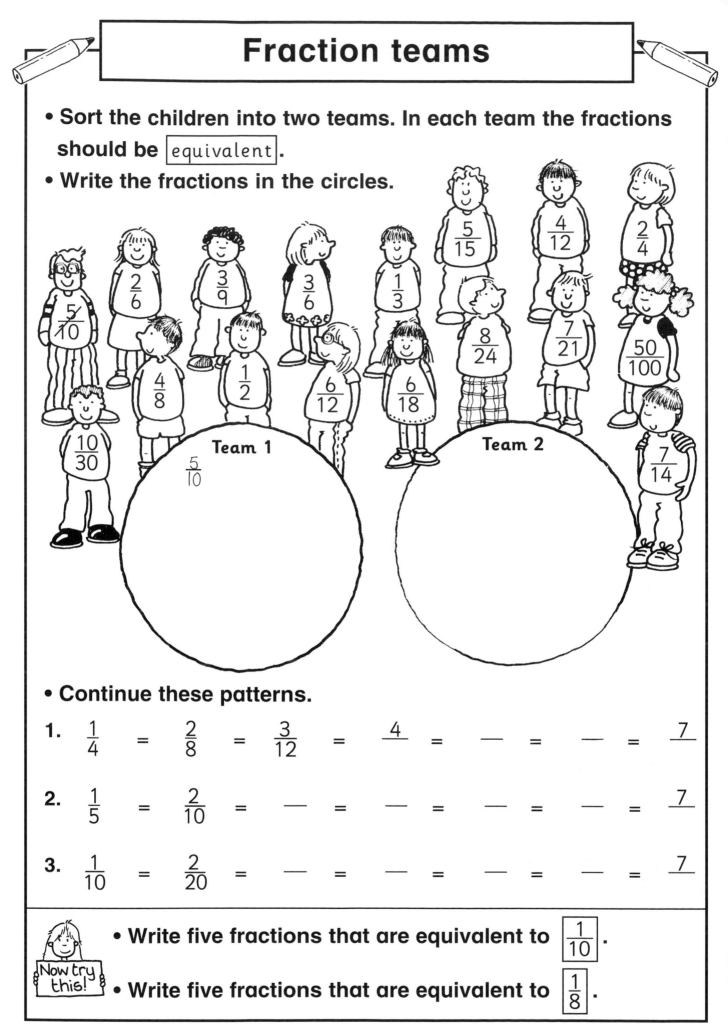

- Continue these patterns.

1. $\dfrac{1}{4}$ = $\dfrac{2}{8}$ = $\dfrac{3}{12}$ = $\dfrac{4}{\rule{1cm}{0.4pt}}$ = $\dfrac{\rule{1cm}{0.4pt}}{\rule{1cm}{0.4pt}}$ = $\dfrac{\rule{1cm}{0.4pt}}{\rule{1cm}{0.4pt}}$ = $\dfrac{7}{\rule{1cm}{0.4pt}}$

2. $\dfrac{1}{5}$ = $\dfrac{2}{10}$ = $\dfrac{\rule{1cm}{0.4pt}}{\rule{1cm}{0.4pt}}$ = $\dfrac{\rule{1cm}{0.4pt}}{\rule{1cm}{0.4pt}}$ = $\dfrac{\rule{1cm}{0.4pt}}{\rule{1cm}{0.4pt}}$ = $\dfrac{\rule{1cm}{0.4pt}}{\rule{1cm}{0.4pt}}$ = $\dfrac{7}{\rule{1cm}{0.4pt}}$

3. $\dfrac{1}{10}$ = $\dfrac{2}{20}$ = $\dfrac{\rule{1cm}{0.4pt}}{\rule{1cm}{0.4pt}}$ = $\dfrac{\rule{1cm}{0.4pt}}{\rule{1cm}{0.4pt}}$ = $\dfrac{\rule{1cm}{0.4pt}}{\rule{1cm}{0.4pt}}$ = $\dfrac{\rule{1cm}{0.4pt}}{\rule{1cm}{0.4pt}}$ = $\dfrac{7}{\rule{1cm}{0.4pt}}$

Now try this!

- Write five fractions that are equivalent to $\dfrac{1}{10}$.
- Write five fractions that are equivalent to $\dfrac{1}{8}$.

Teachers' note The children may need to use fraction boards or fraction circles to check their answers.

**Developing Numeracy
Numbers and the Number System
Year 5
© A & C Black**

Fraction squares

• **Colour the correct fractions. Then complete the statements.**

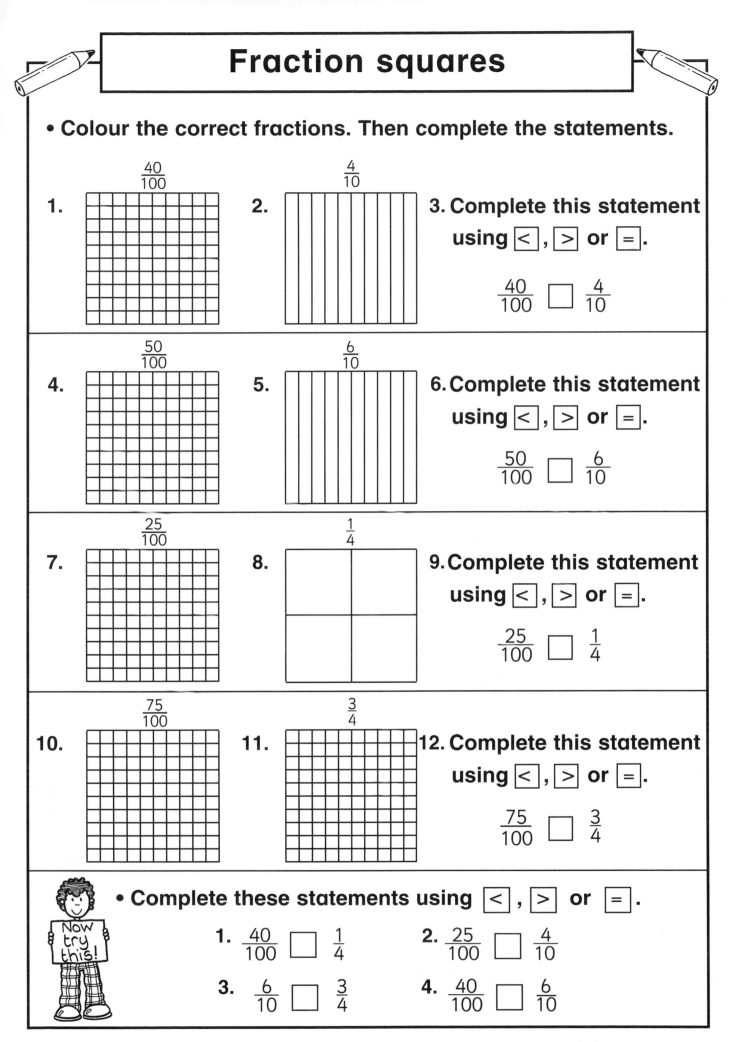

1. $\frac{40}{100}$

2. $\frac{4}{10}$

3. **Complete this statement using** ⌷<⌷ , ⌷>⌷ **or** ⌷=⌷.

   $\frac{40}{100}$ ☐ $\frac{4}{10}$

4. $\frac{50}{100}$

5. $\frac{6}{10}$

6. **Complete this statement using** ⌷<⌷ , ⌷>⌷ **or** ⌷=⌷.

   $\frac{50}{100}$ ☐ $\frac{6}{10}$

7. $\frac{25}{100}$

8. $\frac{1}{4}$

9. **Complete this statement using** ⌷<⌷ , ⌷>⌷ **or** ⌷=⌷.

   $\frac{25}{100}$ ☐ $\frac{1}{4}$

10. $\frac{75}{100}$

11. $\frac{3}{4}$

12. **Complete this statement using** ⌷<⌷ , ⌷>⌷ **or** ⌷=⌷.

    $\frac{75}{100}$ ☐ $\frac{3}{4}$

Now try this!

• **Complete these statements using** ⌷<⌷ , ⌷>⌷ **or** ⌷=⌷.

   1. $\frac{40}{100}$ ☐ $\frac{1}{4}$ 2. $\frac{25}{100}$ ☐ $\frac{4}{10}$

   3. $\frac{6}{10}$ ☐ $\frac{3}{4}$ 4. $\frac{40}{100}$ ☐ $\frac{6}{10}$

Teachers' note Provide the children with a 100-square to reinforce the ideas on this page. Point out to the children that they can use the shaded grids in the main activity to help them complete the extension activity.

Developing Numeracy
Numbers and the Number System
Year 5
© A & C Black

Number ordering game

- **Cut out the cards and spread them out face down.**
- **Take turns to turn over a card.**
- **Put the numbers on the cards in order, starting with the smallest.**
- **Continue until all the cards are used up.**

$2\frac{1}{2}$	$2\frac{3}{4}$	$2\frac{1}{4}$	2
$1\frac{1}{2}$	$1\frac{3}{4}$	$1\frac{1}{4}$	1
$\frac{1}{2}$	$\frac{3}{4}$	$\frac{1}{4}$	0
$3\frac{1}{2}$	$3\frac{3}{4}$	$3\frac{1}{4}$	3
$4\frac{1}{2}$	$4\frac{3}{4}$	$4\frac{1}{4}$	4

Teachers' note This game can be played in pairs. The children could also stick the cards on to a strip of card to make a number line display.

Developing Numeracy
Numbers and the Number System
Year 5
© A & C Black

42

Fraction lines

• **Join the fractions to the correct positions on the number lines.**

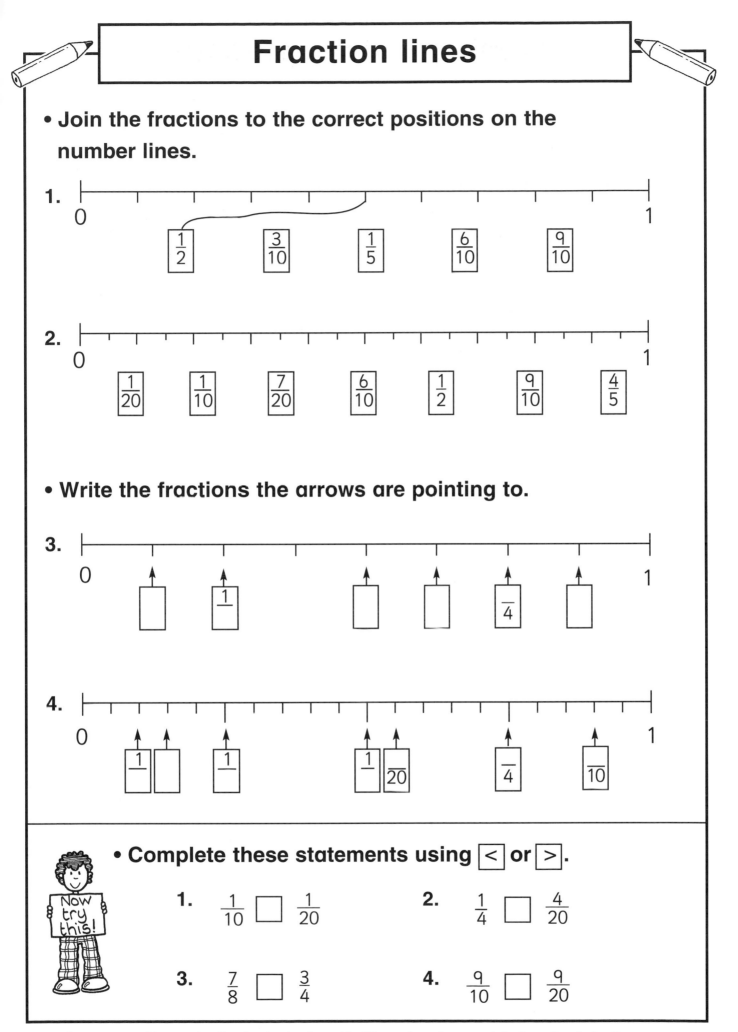

1. 0 ———————————— 1

   $\frac{1}{2}$ $\frac{3}{10}$ $\frac{1}{5}$ $\frac{6}{10}$ $\frac{9}{10}$

2. 0 ———————————— 1

   $\frac{1}{20}$ $\frac{1}{10}$ $\frac{7}{20}$ $\frac{6}{10}$ $\frac{1}{2}$ $\frac{9}{10}$ $\frac{4}{5}$

• **Write the fractions the arrows are pointing to.**

3. 0 ———————————— 1

   ☐ $\frac{1}{}$ ☐   ☐ $\frac{}{4}$ ☐

4. 0 ———————————— 1

   $\frac{1}{}$ ☐ $\frac{1}{}$ $\frac{1}{}\frac{}{20}$ $\frac{}{4}$ $\frac{}{10}$

• **Complete these statements using** ☐< ☐ **or** ☐> ☐ **.**

1. $\frac{1}{10}$ ☐ $\frac{1}{20}$ 2. $\frac{1}{4}$ ☐ $\frac{4}{20}$

3. $\frac{7}{8}$ ☐ $\frac{3}{4}$ 4. $\frac{9}{10}$ ☐ $\frac{9}{20}$

Teachers' note Provide a number line showing fractions with different denominators to help the children complete this activity.

Developing Numeracy
Numbers and the Number System
Year 5
© A & C Black

Dividing game

- **Take turns to roll a dice and move your counter.**
- **Answer the question.**
- **If you get it wrong, go back one space.**

When you land on a shaded space, the answer is a whole number. All the other answers are fractions.

start

one fifth of 15

3 ÷ 4

$\frac{1}{3}$ of 9

9 ÷ 10

one eighth of 16

7 ÷ 8

one seventh of 21

4 ÷ 5

9 ÷ 3

one quarter of 3

one half of 48

$\frac{1}{10}$ of 7

$\frac{1}{10}$ of 40

$\frac{1}{4}$ of 5

$\frac{1}{6}$ of 24

one tenth of 9

$\frac{1}{8}$ of 16

$\frac{1}{8}$ of 7

$\frac{1}{7}$ of 21

$\frac{1}{5}$ of 4

24 ÷ 6

one quarter of 7

40 ÷ 10

one tenth of 7

$\frac{1}{2}$ of 48

$\frac{1}{5}$ of 3

99 ÷ 100

one fifth of 25

$\frac{1}{6}$ of 36

5 ÷ 6

$\frac{1}{9}$ of 18

7 ÷ 10

15 ÷ 5

one tenth of 3

one tenth of 80

one sixth of 5

28 divided by 7

one eighth of 7

$\frac{1}{5}$ of 35

finish

Teachers' note This is a game for two players. The children will need a counter each and a dice, and they should write down their answers. Encourage the children to consider the link between division and fractions.

Developing Numeracy
Numbers and the Number System
Year 5
© A & C Black

44

Flower power

• **Write the missing numbers.**

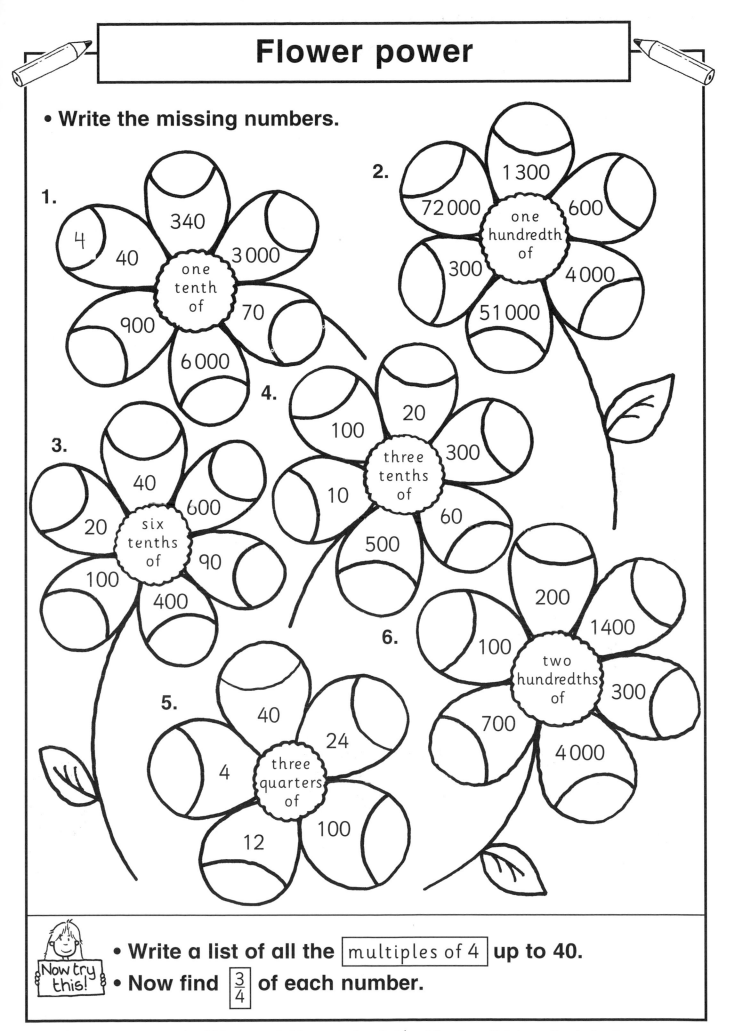

1. *one tenth of*: 4, 40, 340, 3 000, 70, 6 000, 900

2. *one hundredth of*: 1 300, 72 000, 600, 300, 4 000, 51 000

3. *six tenths of*: 40, 600, 20, 90, 100, 400

4. *three tenths of*: 100, 20, 300, 10, 60, 500

5. *three quarters of*: 40, 24, 4, 100, 12

6. *two hundredths of*: 200, 1400, 100, 300, 700, 4 000

• **Write a list of all the** multiples of 4 **up to 40.**
• **Now find** $\frac{3}{4}$ **of each number.**

Teachers' note Encourage the children to use halving methods to find $\frac{1}{4}$ and then to multiply by 3 to find $\frac{3}{4}$.

Developing Numeracy
Numbers and the Number System
Year 5
© A & C Black

Bits and pieces

• **Write the missing measurements.**

1.

120 cm of string

$\frac{1}{4}$ $\frac{3}{4}$ $\frac{1}{6}$

30 cm

2.

36 kg of luggage

$\frac{1}{6}$ $\frac{5}{6}$ $\frac{1}{9}$

3.

200 ml of water

$\frac{1}{10}$ $\frac{2}{10}$ $\frac{9}{10}$

4.

25 kg of potatoes

$\frac{1}{5}$ $\frac{3}{5}$ $\frac{4}{5}$

5.

48 cm of ribbon

$\frac{1}{6}$ $\frac{5}{6}$ $\frac{1}{8}$

6.

800 ml of wine

$\frac{1}{10}$ $\frac{2}{10}$ $\frac{1}{100}$

7.

2000 cm of cotton

$\frac{1}{100}$ $\frac{7}{100}$ $\frac{9}{10}$

8.

70 l of water

$\frac{1}{10}$ $\frac{3}{10}$ $\frac{1}{7}$

9.

40 kg of me!

$\frac{3}{4}$ $\frac{7}{8}$ $\frac{9}{10}$

Teachers' note During the initial whole class activity, the children could predict which of the three fractions will give the smallest and largest measures.

**Developing Numeracy
Numbers and the Number System
Year 5
© A & C Black**

Find the fractions

1. What fraction of 1 metre is

1 cm? $\frac{1}{100}$ 3 cm? _____   27 cm? _____

2. What fraction of 1 centimetre is

1 mm? _____   3 mm? _____   9 mm? _____

3. What fraction of 1 kilometre is

1 m? _____   35 m? _____   750 m? _____

4. What fraction of 1 kilogram is

1 g? _____   7 g? _____   999 g? _____

5. What fraction of 1 litre is

1 ml? _____   95 ml? _____   500 ml? _____

6. What fraction of 1 week is

1 day? _____   3 days? _____   5 days? _____

7. What fraction of 1 day is

1 hour? _____   12 hours? _____   6 hours? _____

Now try this!

• **How many minutes in:**

1. $\frac{1}{60}$ hour? _____   2. $\frac{1}{2}$ hour? _____   3. $\frac{59}{60}$ hour? _____

• **How many seconds in:**

4. $\frac{1}{60}$ minute? _____   5. $\frac{1}{4}$ minute? _____   6. $\frac{47}{60}$ minute? _____

Teachers' note As a further activity, the children could explore fractions of a year, in terms of months, days and weeks.

Developing Numeracy
Numbers and the Number System
Year 5
© A & C Black

Who's telling the truth?

Chirag   Louis

Chirag has two stickers for every one that Louis has.

• Write true or false next to each statement.

1. I've got half as many as Louis. _____

2. No, I've got half as many as Chirag. _____

3. So I've got twice as many as Louis. _____

4. Chirag has 8, so I must have 16. _____

5. No, I've got 8 so Louis must have 4. _____

6. When Chirag had 20, I had 10. _____

7. When I had 14, Louis had 28! _____

Now Chirag has three **stickers for every one that Louis has.**

• **Write four true statements.**

Teachers' note The activity could be extended further by asking the children to write their own true or false statements based on different ratios, for example, two for every three or three for every five.

**Developing Numeracy
Numbers and the Number System
Year 5
© A & C Black**

Special offers

1. The supermarket has this special offer:

> ✧☆ Get one **FREE** item ✧☆
> for every two items you buy!

- The list shows what Nina bought. Complete the chart to show how many extra items she got free.

| 4 bars of soap |
| 8 packets of crisps |
| 2 toothbrushes |
| 10 batteries |
| 6 toilet rolls |

Free items	
2	bars of soap
	packets of crisps
	toothbrush
	batteries
	toilet rolls

2. The stationer's has this special offer:

> Get two **FREE** items for every
> five pounds you spend!

- The list shows what Sam spent. Complete the chart to show how many extra items he got free.

| £5 on pens |
| £15 on tapes |
| £30 on batteries |
| £10 on pencils |
| £25 on books |

Free items
pens
tapes
batteries
pencils
books

Now try this!

- Write a special offer of your own.
- Write a shopping list and ask a friend to work out what items they will get free.

Teachers' note Encourage the children to look out for similar offers in shops.

Developing Numeracy
Numbers and the Number System
Year 5
© A & C Black

Chocolate chunks

• **Write the amounts of chocolate as decimals.**

This is one whole bar of chocolate.

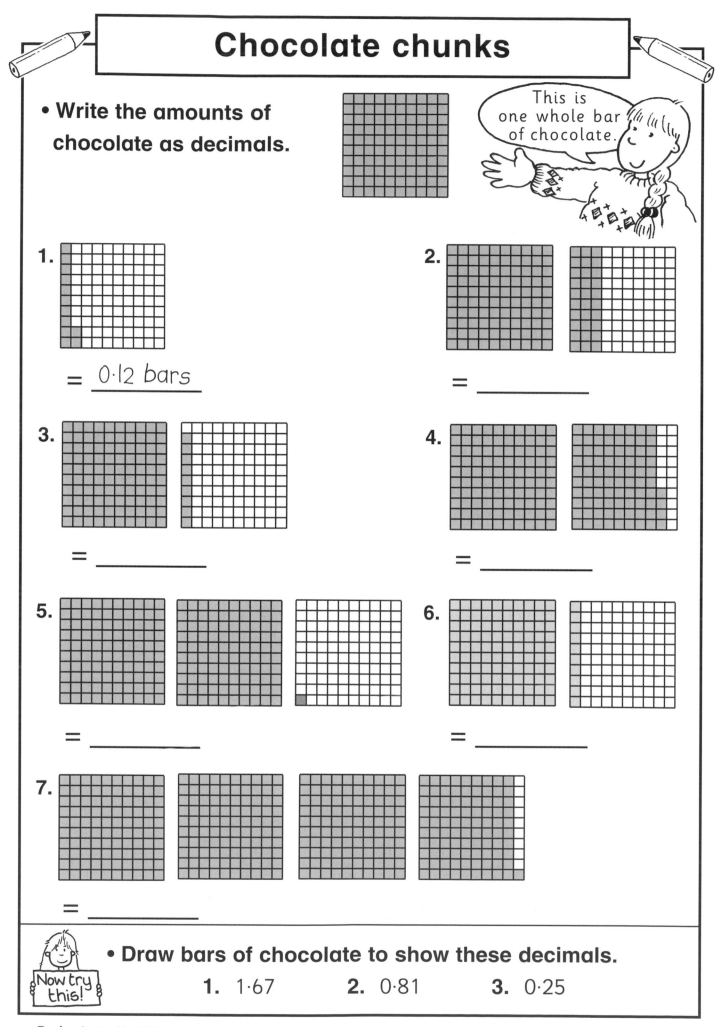

1. = _0·12 bars_

2. = _____

3. = _____

4. = _____

5. = _____

6. = _____

7. = _____

• **Draw bars of chocolate to show these decimals.**

1. 1·67   **2.** 0·81   **3.** 0·25

Now try this!

Teachers' note Use 100-squares to reinforce these ideas and provide further practice.

Developing Numeracy
Numbers and the Number System
Year 5
© A & C Black

Gardeners' world

- **Colour the leaf that shows the value of the underlined digit.**

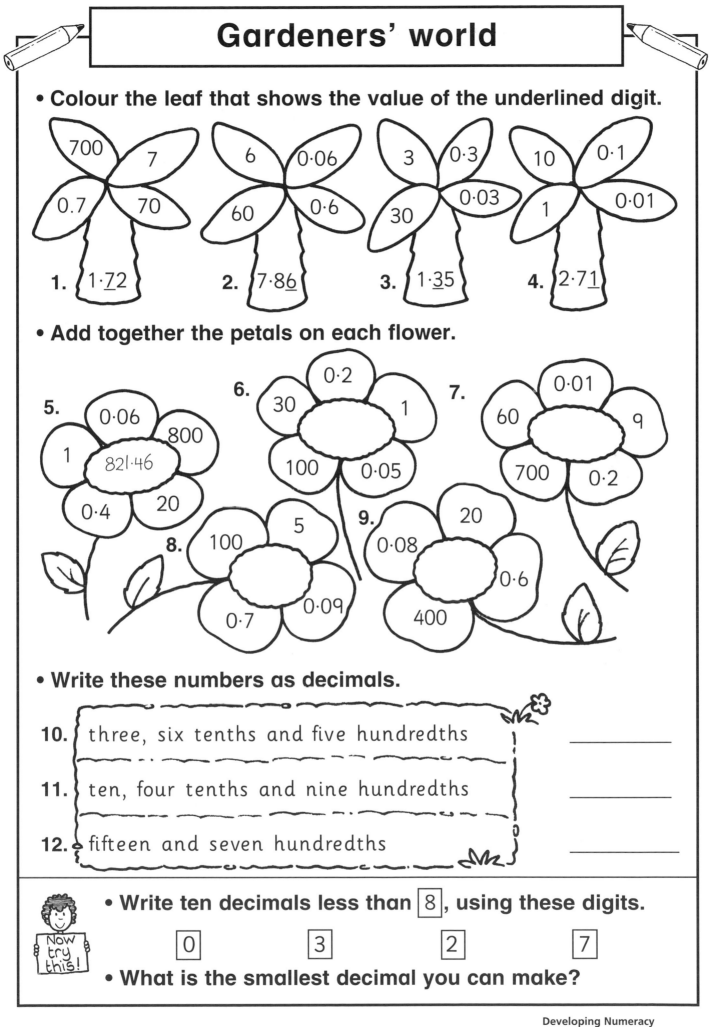

700   7
0.7   70
1. 1·7<u>2</u>

6   0·06
60   0·6
2. 7·8<u>6</u>

3   0·3
30   0·03
3. 1·<u>3</u>5

10   0·1
1   0·01
4. 2·7<u>1</u>

- **Add together the petals on each flower.**

5.
0·06
1   800
821·46
0·4   20

6.
0·2
30   1
100   0·05

7.
0·01
60   9
700   0·2

8.
100   5
0·7   0·09

9.
20
0·08
0·6
400

- **Write these numbers as decimals.**

10. three, six tenths and five hundredths _____

11. ten, four tenths and nine hundredths _____

12. fifteen and seven hundredths _____

- **Write ten decimals less than** $\boxed{8}$ **, using these digits.**

$\boxed{0}$ $\boxed{3}$ $\boxed{2}$ $\boxed{7}$

- **What is the smallest decimal you can make?**

Developing Numeracy
Numbers and the Number System
Year 5
© A & C Black

Colour by decimals

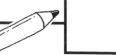

• **Use the key to colour the picture. Use a different colour for each decimal fraction.**

Example: 7·4 has four tenths, so colour it blue.

three tenths	yellow	eight hundredths	brown
one unit	red	six units	black
six hundredths	green	nine tenths	white
four tenths	blue	five tens	orange

Teachers' note As an extension activity, the children could list the numbers they have coloured which show the different decimal fractions.

**Developing Numeracy
Numbers and the Number System
Year 5
© A & C Black**

All at sea

• **Write the correct decimal on each buoy.**

1. $1.47 + 0.1 = 1.57$ 2. $3.71 + \boxed{} = 3.79$

3. $0.8 + \boxed{} = 0.86$ 4. $2.73 + \boxed{} = 2.93$

5. $0.05 + \boxed{} = 3.05$ 6. $5.15 + \boxed{} = 5.95$

7. $6.94 + \boxed{} = 7.04$ 8. $8.97 + \boxed{} = 9.00$

• **Write the correct number on each buoy.**

9. $1.6 \times \boxed{} = 16$ 10. $4.2 \times \boxed{} = 42$

11. $3.71 \times \boxed{} = 371$ 12. $6.55 \times \boxed{} = 65.5$

Now try this!

• **Key in $\boxed{3.45}$ on a calculator.**

• **In one step, add a decimal to make $\boxed{4.69}$.**

• **Which decimal did you add?** _____

Developing Numeracy
Numbers and the Number System
Year 5
© A & C Black

Hang out the washing

- **Write the decimals on the clothes in order, starting with the smallest number.**

1.

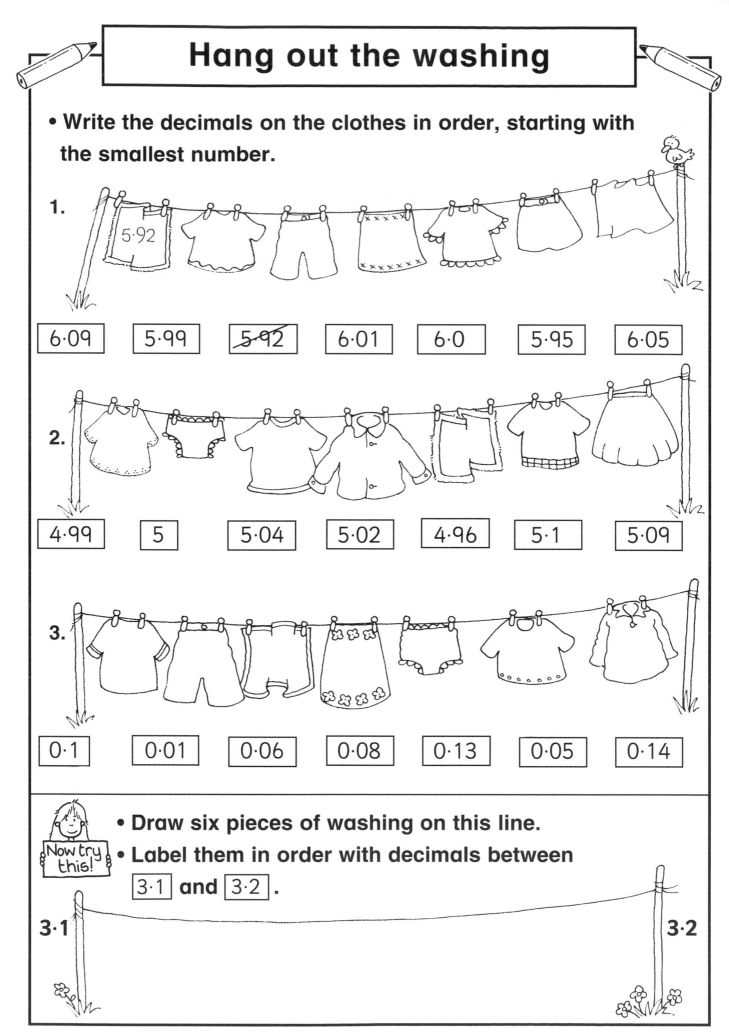

| 6·09 | 5·99 | ~~5·92~~ | 6·01 | 6·0 | 5·95 | 6·05 |

2.

| 4·99 | 5 | 5·04 | 5·02 | 4·96 | 5·1 | 5·09 |

3.

| 0·1 | 0·01 | 0·06 | 0·08 | 0·13 | 0·05 | 0·14 |

Now try this!

- **Draw six pieces of washing on this line.**
- **Label them in order with decimals between** 3·1 **and** 3·2 .

3·1   **3·2**

Teachers' note As a further extension activity, ask the children to write five decimals in order between 0 and 0.09.

Developing Numeracy
Numbers and the Number System
Year 5
© A & C Black

Decimal dominoes

- **Cut out the dominoes and share them out.**
- **Player 1 puts a domino face up.**
- **The next player puts down a domino with an equivalent quantity, and so on.**

> Only cut along the dotted lines.

3·5 m	6500 g	8·5 kg	6500 ml	9·5 kg	8500 ml
1·5 cm	2500 g	6·5 kg	750 c m	9·5 l	15 mm
8·5 l	4500 ml	5·5 km	3500 g	6·5 l	7500 g
7·5 kg	65 mm	2·5 kg	45 mm	1·5 kg	450 c m
4·5 m	9500 ml	4·5 l	95 mm	3·5 kg	25 mm
7·5 m	850 cm	6·5 cm	5500 m	9·5 cm	8500 mg
2·5 cm	1500 g	8·5 m	9500 g	4·5 cm	350 cm

Teachers' note This is a game for two or more players. Photocopy this page on to A3 card and ensure that the children understand how to play dominoes. The cards can also be used as a whole class activity, where each child has one card. Read out one quantity and encourage the children to continue the loop until all the quantities have been read out.

Developing Numeracy
Numbers and the Number System
Year 5
© A & C Black

Right or wrong?

• Can you mark and correct Urvi's homework for her?

Name: __Urvi__

Homework

Rounding to the nearest whole number

1. 2·6 → 3 ✓
   2̶ ✗

2. 1·7 → 6

3. 5·9 → 6

4. 4·2 → 4

5. 3·7 → 3

6. 2·5 → 2

7. 8·7 → 9

8. 9·9 → 9

9. 8·4 → 9

10. 6·1 → 6

11. 7·2 → 8

12. 5·5 → 5

13. 7·8 → 9

14. 2·4 → 2

15. 3·5 → 4

16. 22·4 → 22

17. 16·9 → 17

18. 15·2 → 14

19. 123·1 → 123

20. 64·7 → 65

21. 99·6 → 99

22. 81·1 → 81

23. 11·5 → 11

24. 164·5 → 165

25. 342·6 → 343

26. 841·0 → 841

27. 666·2 → 6·67

28. 812·5 → 813

29. 695·4 → 695

30. 1000·5 → 1001

Now try this!

• Write all the decimals with one decimal place that round to $\boxed{4}$.

Examples: 3·5, 3·6

Teachers' note Ensure that the children correct any wrong answers on Urvi's homework. Remind them that 2·5 is rounded up to the next whole number.

Developing Numeracy
Numbers and the Number System
Year 5
© A & C Black

Sports round-up

- Round the decimal on each golf ball to the nearest whole number. Join it to the correct hole.

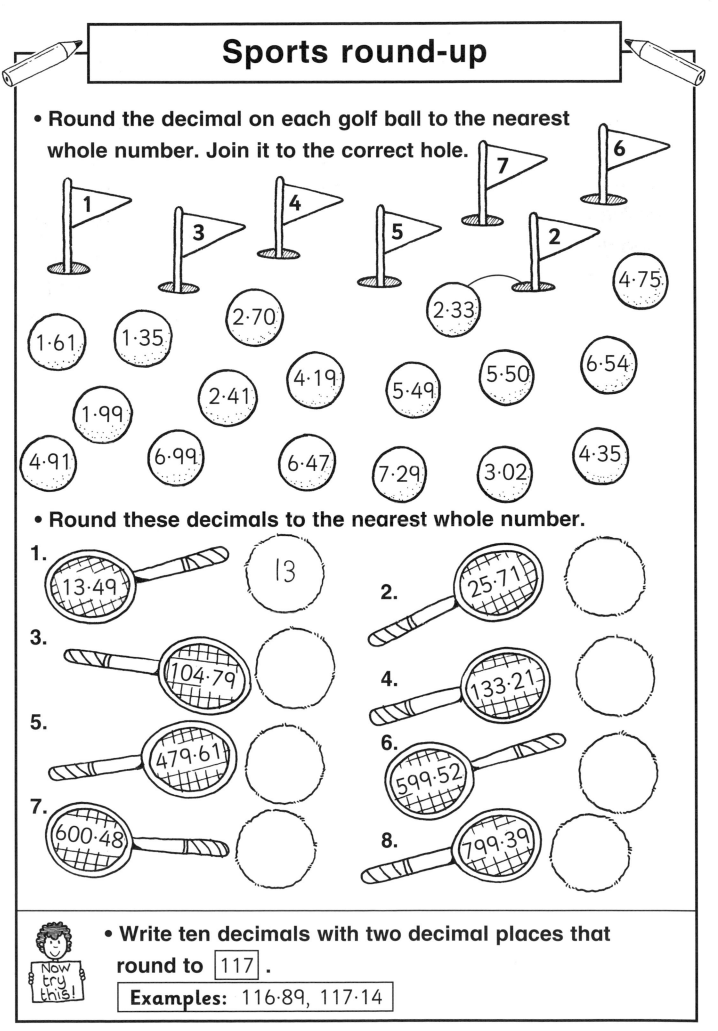

- Round these decimals to the nearest whole number.

1. 13·49   13

2. 25·71

3. 104·79

4. 133·21

5. 479·61

6. 599·52

7. 600·48

8. 799·39

- Write ten decimals with two decimal places that round to 117 .

Examples: 116·89, 117·14

Teachers' note Remind the children that 0·5 rounds up to the next whole number.

Developing Numeracy
Numbers and the Number System
Year 5
© A & C Black

Counter switch puzzle

- **Put a counter on each** start **hexagon.**
- **With your partner, move the counters at the same time to hexagons with the same value as each other. You can only move to touching spaces.** **Example:** $\langle$ 0·75 $\rangle$ = $\langle \frac{3}{4} \rangle$
- **Can you both reach the opposite side?**

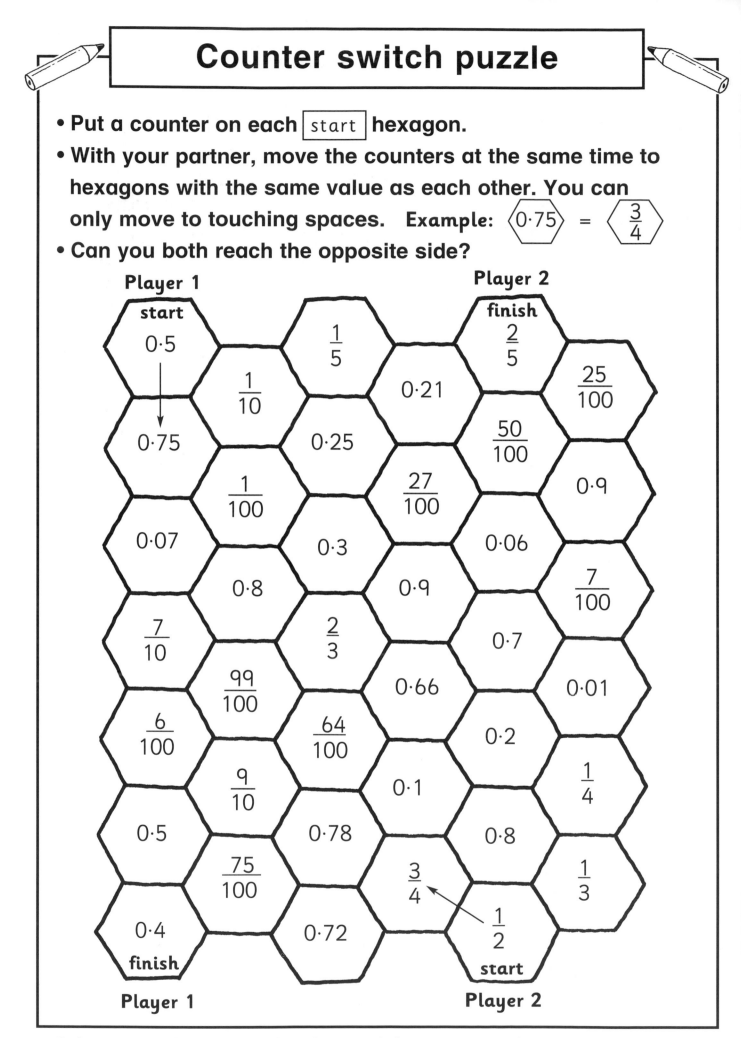

Teachers' note Ensure that the children work together to move both counters on to equivalent fractions or decimals.

Developing Numeracy
Numbers and the Number System
Year 5
© A & C Black

Percentage spotting

- **Complete these clothing labels, making sure that they total 100%.**

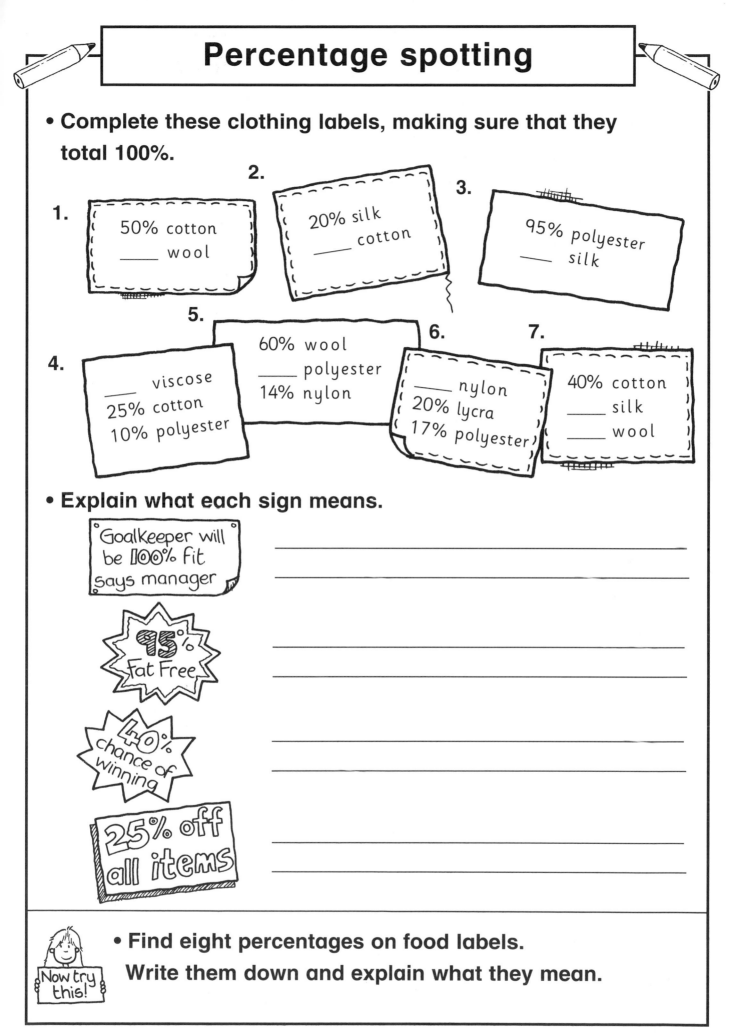

1. 50% cotton
   ___ wool

2. 20% silk
   ___ cotton

3. 95% polyester
   ___ silk

4. ___ viscose
   25% cotton
   10% polyester

5. 60% wool
   ___ polyester
   14% nylon

6. ___ nylon
   20% lycra
   17% polyester

7. 40% cotton
   ___ silk
   ___ wool

- **Explain what each sign means.**

Goalkeeper will be 100% fit says manager

_____
_____

75% Fat Free

_____
_____

40% chance of winning

_____
_____

25% off all items

_____
_____

Now try this!

- **Find eight percentages on food labels.**
  Write them down and explain what they mean.

Teachers' note For the extension activity, provide the children with food packaging and magazines. Alternatively, the activity could be given as homework.

**Developing Numeracy
Numbers and the Number System
Year 5
© A & C Black**

Percentage pictures

• **What percentage is shaded?**

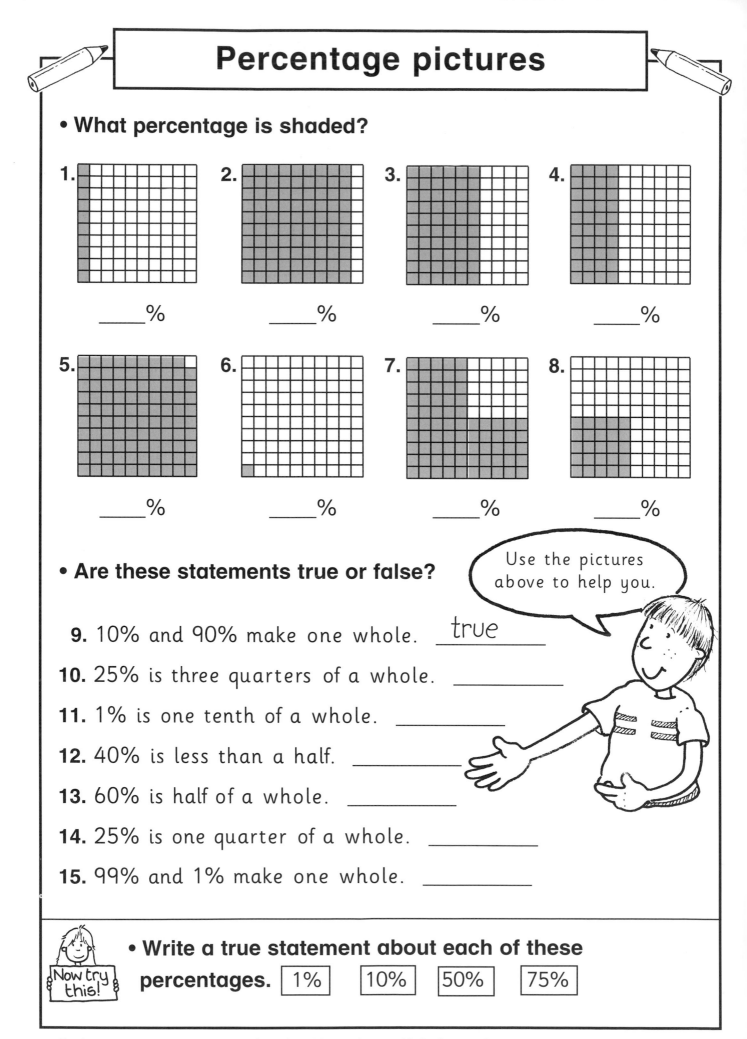

1. _____ %

2. _____ %

3. _____ %

4. _____ %

5. _____ %

6. _____ %

7. _____ %

8. _____ %

• **Are these statements true or false?**

Use the pictures above to help you.

9. 10% and 90% make one whole. ___true___

10. 25% is three quarters of a whole. _____

11. 1% is one tenth of a whole. _____

12. 40% is less than a half. _____

13. 60% is half of a whole. _____

14. 25% is one quarter of a whole. _____

15. 99% and 1% make one whole. _____

Now try this!

• **Write a true statement about each of these percentages.** 1% | 10% | 50% | 75%

Teachers' note Use 100-squares to reinforce these ideas and to provide further practice.

**Developing Numeracy
Numbers and the Number System
Year 5
© A & C Black**

Percentage work-out

- **What is 50% of:**

1. 26? [13]   **2.** 32? [ ]   **3.** 88? [ ]   **4.** 124? [ ]

5. 400? [ ]   **6.** 360? [ ]   **7.** 500? [ ]   **8.** 1000? [ ]

- **What is 25% of:**

9. 4? [ ]   **10.** 16? [ ]   **11.** 40? [ ]

12. 200? [ ]   **13.** 320? [ ]   **14.** 600? [ ]

To find 25%, halve the number and halve it again.

- **What is 10% of:**

15. 60? [ ]   **16.** 90? [ ]   **17.** 110? [ ]

18. 340? [ ]   **19.** 6900? [ ]   **20.** 1000? [ ]   **21.** 52 000? [ ]

75% is the same as three quarters.

- **What is 75% of:**

22. 40? [ ]   **23.** 16? [ ]   **24.** 24? [ ]

25. 200? [ ]   **26.** 600? [ ]   **27.** 888? [ ]

- **What is 1% of:**

28. 600? [ ]   **29.** 3000? [ ]   **30.** 17 000? [ ]

Now try this!

- **Write five prices in pounds.**

  Example: £20

- **Ask a friend to work out the new price when there is a**

  50% discount   10% discount

Teachers' note Encourage the children to work mentally when finding these percentages.

Developing Numeracy
Numbers and the Number System
Year 5
© A & C Black

61

Plot the percentage

- **Take turns to roll a dice and move forward.**
- **Write down the answer to each question that you land on.**
- **Your partner can check your answers on a calculator.**

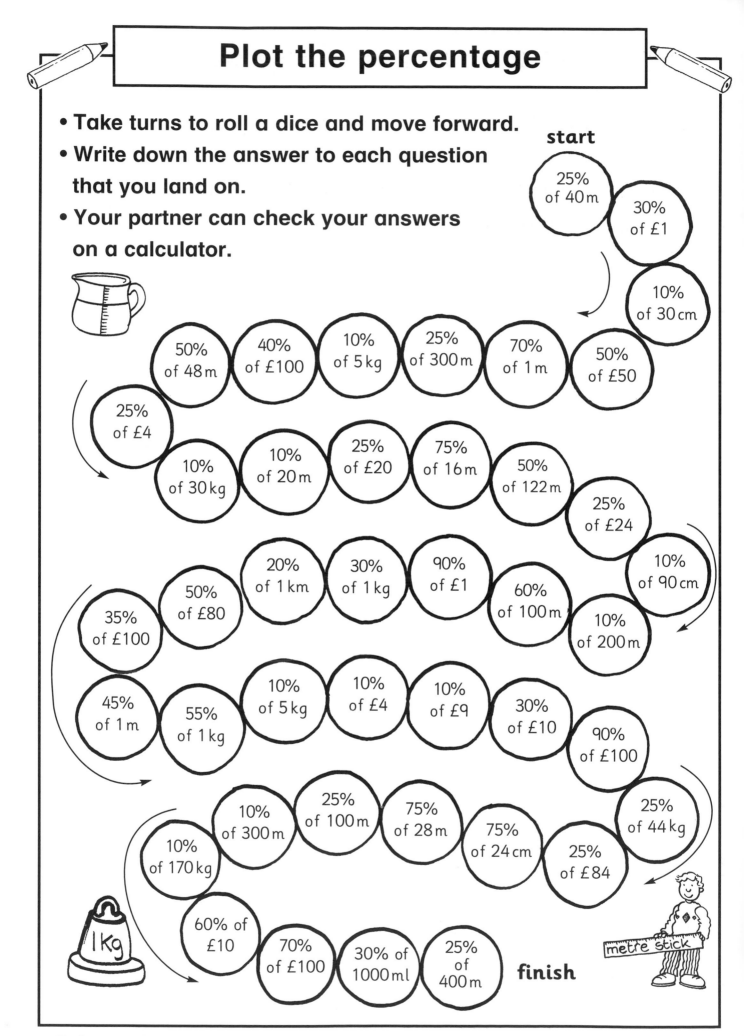

start

25% of 40m

30% of £1

10% of 30cm

50% of 48m

40% of £100

10% of 5kg

25% of 300m

70% of 1m

50% of £50

25% of £4

10% of 30kg

10% of 20m

25% of £20

75% of 16m

50% of 122m

25% of £24

10% of 90cm

35% of £100

50% of £80

20% of 1km

30% of 1kg

90% of £1

60% of 100m

10% of 200m

45% of 1m

55% of 1kg

10% of 5kg

10% of £4

10% of £9

30% of £10

90% of £100

25% of 44kg

10% of 170kg

10% of 300m

25% of 100m

75% of 28m

75% of 24cm

25% of £84

60% of £10

70% of £100

30% of 1000ml

25% of 400m

finish

metre stick

Teachers' note The children should play this game in pairs. They will need a counter each, a dice and a calculator. As an extension activity, the children could be asked to find the largest and smallest answers on this page (disregarding the units of measurement).

Developing Numeracy
Numbers and the Number System
Year 5
© A & C Black

Percentage matching game

- **Cut along the dotted lines to make 16 triangles.**
  Share them between two players. Player 1 puts down
  a triangle. Player 2 puts another triangle next to it so
  that the touching sides are equivalent, and so on.

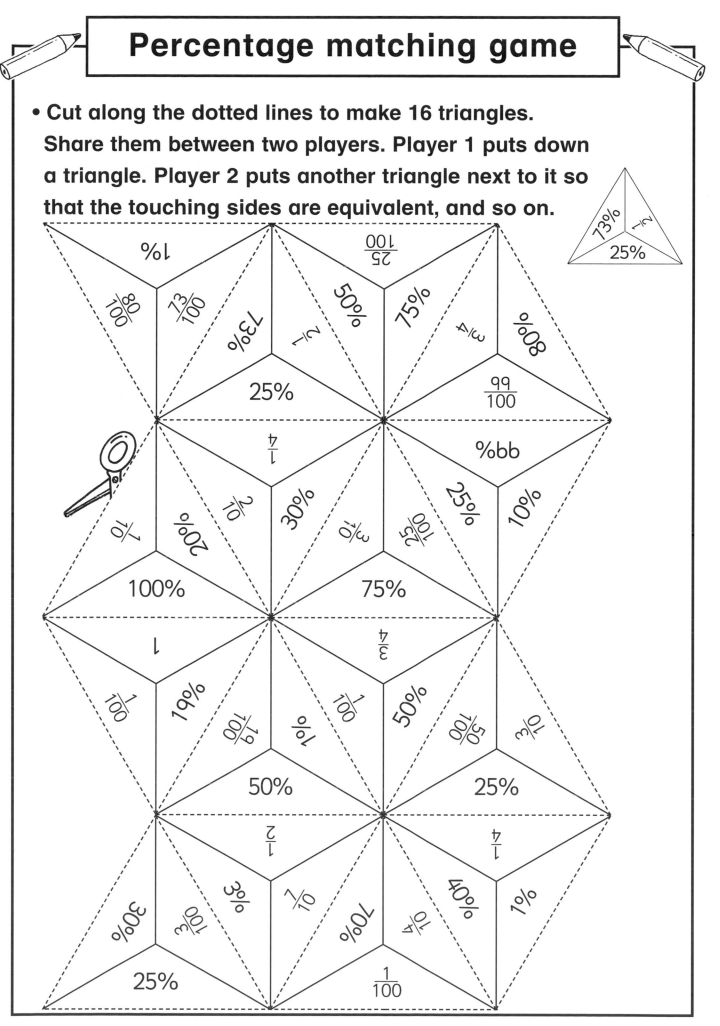

Teachers' note To extend the activity, the numbers on the triangles could be masked and a new
set of numbers substituted before photocopying.

Developing Numeracy
Numbers and the Number System
Year 5
© A & C Black

Link-ball

- **Join the balls that show** equivalent **values. There are seven groups.**

Use a different colour for each group.

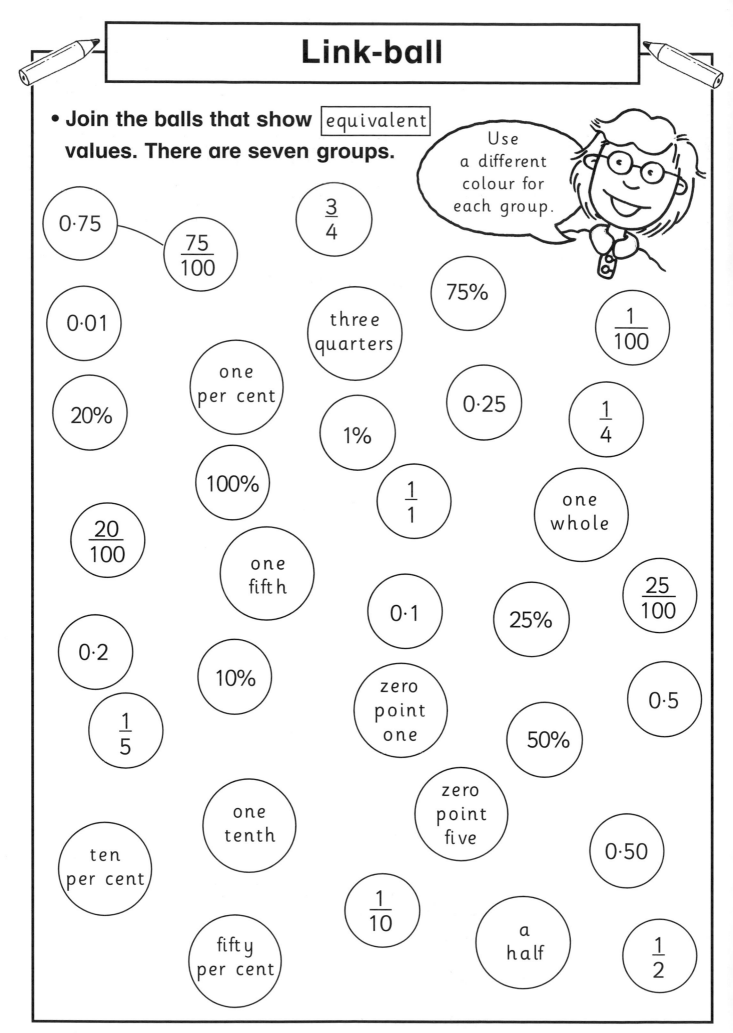

Teachers' note Discuss the different forms of representing the same proportion, for example, using fractions, decimals and percentages.

Developing Numeracy
Numbers and the Number System
Year 5
© A & C Black